FIRST
GREAT
WESTERN

GATEWAY TO THE WEST

FIRST GREAT WESTERN

GATEWAY TO THE WEST

JOHN BALMFORTH

FONTHILL

Fonthill Media Limited
Fonthill Media LLC
www.fonthillmedia.com
office@fonthillmedia.com

First published in the United Kingdom and the United States of America 2015

British Library Cataloguing in Publication Data:
A catalogue record for this book is available from the British Library

Copyright © John Balmforth 2015

ISBN 978-1-78155-004-5

Typeset in 10pt on 13pt Sabon
Printed and bound in England

Contents

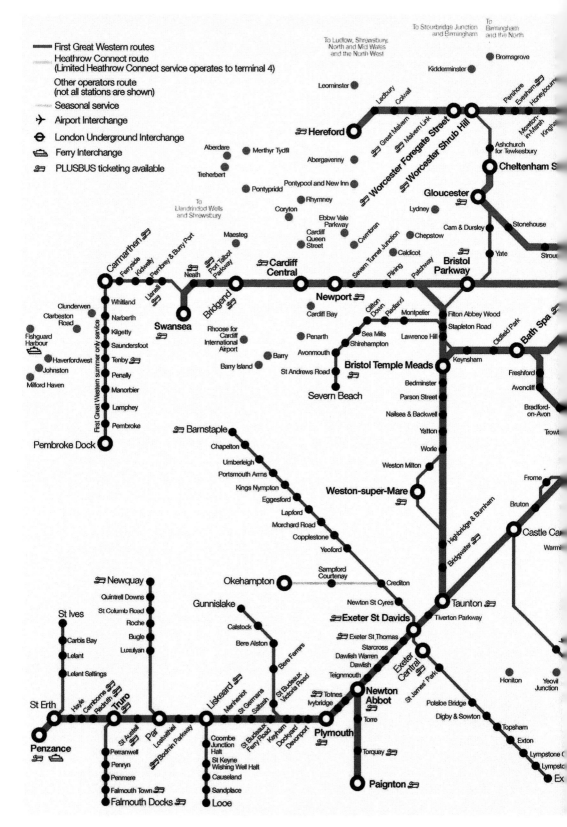

First Great Western route network. (*Courtesy First Great Western*)

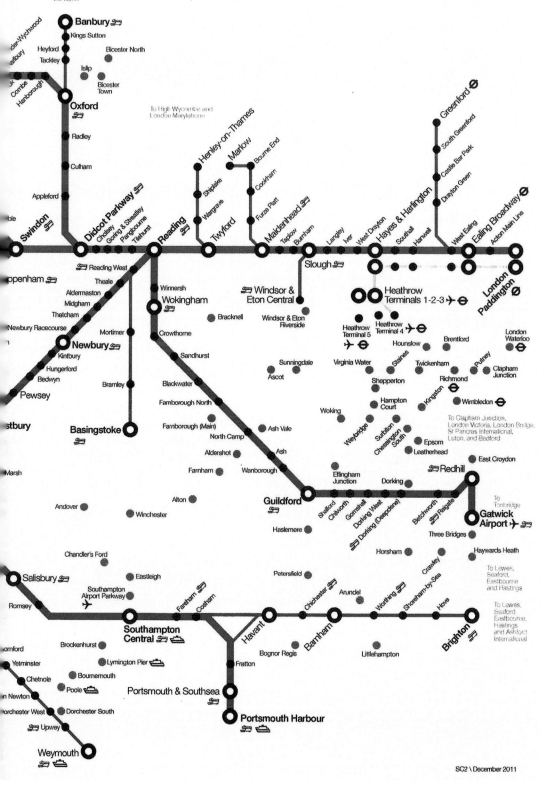

SC2 \ December 2011

Class 180 Adelante No. 180103 approaches Slough at speed on 25 February 2005, when forming a service from Cheltenham Spa. (*Brian Morrison*)

This book is dedicated to my grandchildren who are a constant source of inspiration: Penelope May Balmforth, Lewis Albert Balmforth, Charlie Jack O'Hare, and Poppy Jane Mitchell.

Acknowledgements

I am extremely grateful to my wife Shirley and my friend Alun Caddy for their tireless work proof reading, and to my friend Allan Stokes for his assistance on countless research trips. Without their help this book would never have got to the publication stage.

I also acknowledge the help given by the following: Stuart Baker; Brian Clark, Driver Simulator Manager, First Great Western; Vicky Cropper, Communications Co-ordinator, First Great Western; Lizzie Dearn, Service Team Leader, Night Riviera sleeper, First Great Western; First Great Western; Richard Gibson, CrossCountry Trains; Mark Hopwood, Managing Director, First Great Western; Jane Jones, External Relations Manager, First Great Western; Jenny Mitchell; Alan Norton, *Night Riviera* sleeper crew, First Great Western; Colin Page, Depot Manager, First Great Western, Laira (Plymouth) T&RSMD; and Jade Winn, *Night Riviera* sleeper crew, First Great Western. I'd also like to thank all the photographers who have allowed their work to be used in this book without charge. If I have overlooked anyone please accept my apologies as it was not intentional.

An exciting part of the research undertaken for this book was the privilege of being allowed a ride in the cab of an HST between Plymouth and Taunton which, of course, included travel along the sea wall at Dawlish. Travel along the sea wall section of the line is always wonderful even from within the carriages, but the driver's eye view is incredible. I am extremely grateful to Brian Payne (driver competence manager) who organised the trip and also to drivers Andy Stewart (Plymouth depot) and Chris Meads (Exeter depot) for allowing me in their cab. I was properly supervised at all times by Brian and some of the photographs included in the book give an insight into life in the driver's cab. I also wish to record my thanks to FGW for allowing me the privilege of sampling both the sleeper and Pullman diner services.

Abbreviations

ANG	Angel Trains
BR	British Rail
CSD	Carriage Siding Depot
DfT	Department for Transport
DMCL	Driving Motor Composite Lavatory
DMS	Driving Motor Standard
DMSL	Driving Motor Standard Lavatory
DMU	Diesel Multiple Unit
DMUD	Diesel Multiple Unit Depot
EU	European Union
FGP	FirstGroup
FGW	First Great Western
FGWL	First Great Western Link
GNER	Great North Eastern Railway
GRT	Grampian Regional Transport
GWR	Great Western Railway
HLOS	High Level Output Specification
hp	Horsepower
HSTMD	High-speed Train Maintenance Depot
IEP	InterCity Express Programme
ITT	Invitation to Tender
Kw	Kilowatts
LNWR	London North Western Railway
LTS	London Tilbury & Southend
MBO	Management–buy-out
MFL	Motor First Lavatory
MS	Motor Standard
MSL	Motor Standard Lavatory
MSLRB	Motor Standard Lavatory Restaurant Buffet
NEEC	National Express East Coast
NR	Network Rail

OPRAF	Office of Passenger Rail Franchising
ORR	Office of Rail Regulation
PIN	Personal Identification Number
PTR	Porterbrook Leasing
ROSCO	Rolling Stock Operating Company
SRA	Strategic Rail Authority
TRSMD	Traction & Rolling Stock Maintenance Depot
TOC	Train Operating Company
TOPS	Total Operations Processing System
TSR	Temporary Speed Restriction
WCML	West Coast Main Line

Foreword
The Great Western Network

Mark Hopwood, Managing Director, First Great Western

The Great Western has a rich heritage dating back to 1833, when the company was founded at a public meeting in Bristol. With the city very much seen as Britain's second port, a railway line to London was fundamental to its future; at the age of just 29, Isambard Kingdom Brunel was appointed engineer.

The resultant railway was ahead of its time and exploited new technology—which is what we are doing today, building on and surpassing the engineering feats of almost 175 years ago. At First Great Western we are pleased to run a business with such a strong association with Brunel's legacy.

The growth in the number of passengers using rail services has been one of the great success stories of the Great Western. I don't think that Brunel ever imagined that trains on this network would cover 70 million miles and carry almost 100 million passengers a year.

Since 2006, when First Great Western took over the Great Western franchise, a comprehensive £80 million re-engineering programme to replace ageing engines in our high-speed train fleet has been central to our improvement plans. These works were essential to improve the reliability, efficiency, and service life of the classic Intercity 125 vehicles.

I am very proud of the fact that we now have the most high-speed trains operating the Great Western network since it was built, and with increased frequencies. More than 170 new rolling stock vehicles were introduced between 2006 and 2012 through our work with the Department for Transport. To increase peak time capacity into and out of London by 9 per cent, our team secured forty-eight additional carriages in 2011 by converting disused former buffet cars.

But much more visible and important to our customers was a £65 million investment to provide new, high-quality interiors for the 400 carriages in the high-speed train fleet, allowing customers to travel in greater comfort than their predecessors.

Alongside our high-speed services, some of the fastest growing and most reliable of all our services are community rail lines, which have shown the value of local services. I am delighted to say that between 2002 and 2013, passenger journeys on the Truro to Falmouth branch line alone increased by 209 per cent.

Looking to the future, government investment in the Great Western is set to transform Brunel's greatest achievements through First Great Western. The electrification of the Great Western mainline will modernise the famous railway with re-signalling, new rolling stock, and station upgrades, paving the way for faster, more reliable services.

Unimagined by Brunel, new electric and dual-mode Intercity Express Trains (replacing Intercity 125 diesel locomotives) have a capability of 140 mph. Filled with the latest technology, they will allow passengers to browse the web, read emails, or simply catch up with friends online as they travel between locations quicker than ever before.

While much was achieved on God's Wonderful Railway in Brunel's time, there is still much to do. The network's longer-term future is very promising if we at First Great Western, committed to supporting the communities we serve, continue to take up the challenge.

Introduction

First Group plc is one of the largest bus/rail operators in the world, and with revenues in excess of £6 billion it is well placed to be the parent company of First Great Western (FGW). Its rail passenger operations encompass the franchises for Greater Western, First Great Western Link (previously Thames Trains), and Wessex Trains, all three now branded as First Great Western, First Capital Connect, Scotrail, and in partnership with Keolis, TransPennine Express, together with an 80 per cent controlling interest in open-access operator Hull Trains. It also operates Croydon Tramlink on behalf of London Transport.

Once the UK government had decided the country's rail network should be privatised by 1996, the railways to the South and West of England and those into South Wales began falling into the hands of private operators. Today's franchise is operated by First Great Western, but those railways have their roots in the nineteenth century, stretching back to 31 August 1835 when the original Great Western Railway Act was passed by Parliament. Isambard Kingdom Brunel is known to have described the Act as 'the finest work in England'. He may well have been right, although the 7-foot-¼-inch broad gauge he adopted failed because the rest of the UK's railways were being built to a 4-foot-8½-inch gauge. His Great Western Railway (GWR) is often described as 'God's Wonderful Railway' by its followers or even the 'Great Way Round' by its detractors, but whatever your viewpoint, it cannot be denied that it left a terrific legacy for the network operated today by First Great Western. Passengers are still able to see much of Brunel's work as they traverse the route in the comfort of the modern trains; perhaps some of the most notable examples are the Clifton Suspension Bridge at Bristol (visible on the right-hand side of trains travelling west shortly after departure from Temple Meads station), the Royal Albert Bridge over the River Tamar at Saltash, the preserved Pumping House at Starcross which powered his atmospheric railway (one of Brunel's few failures), and the famous flat arch bridge over the River Thames at Maidenhead, but there are many others.

The First Great Western story illustrates the difficulties faced by the modern rail industry in the UK. Any bidder for a rail franchise today faces very high costs in just preparing the bid, with no guarantee that it will be successful. Franchise incumbents who have performed well are likely to be invited to bid but cannot be sure of making a winning bid either. Those that are successful, as First Great Western were, may well find that the franchise they are bidding for has had its boundaries adjusted, sometimes causing a loss of income from routes removed to other franchises (although the reverse can also occur), or that difficulties arise from a mixture of the type of services required. First Great Western is a good illustration of this insomuch that it changed from being a mainly high-speed, long-distance operator to one with local, suburban, and regional services added to the previous service it provided.

First Great Western now has a reputation as one of the UK's leading train operating companies (TOC), but life has not always been easy. As we shall see, the new franchise inherited a number of problems; Mark Hopwood was brought in first as Performance Director and shortly afterwards was promoted to Managing Director, with a remit to take the company back to the 'top of the league' of train operators. Educated at the Royal Grammar School, High Wycombe, he went on to gain a BA (Hons) degree in politics from the University of Essex. Steeped in railway experience and supported by an excellent team, he has led the company from being one of the poorest performing operators to being one of the best and most successful. It is a story well worth reading.

John Balmforth
Halesowen
January 2015

Pictured in October 2013 from the window of a FGW high-speed train is one of Brunel's greatest works: his rail bridge across the River Tamar at Saltash. The lettering on the bridge towers pays the great engineer a simple tribute, 'I. K. Brunel Engineer 1859'. (*Alun J. Caddy*)

This Class 180 Adelante unit is seen crossing the River Thames on 31 August 2012. The sleek lines of the driving cab almost match those of the bridge arch. (*Courtesy of First Great Western Photo Archive*)

Three modes of travel are seen parallel in this driver's eye view—road, rail, and sea—as power car No. 43025 approaches the pumping house built for Brunel's atmospheric railway at Starcross travelling at 75 mph *en route* to London Paddington on 24 April 2013. (*John Balmforth*)

1

Privatisation of the UK's Railways: The Background

The Conservative Party won the 1992 General Election with a mandate that the country's main line railway system should pass into private ownership, although that did not indicate in what form, nor did it give any inkling as to how the network should be divided up. Many felt that it should follow the same principle used in the sell-off of the utility companies, or perhaps a return to four companies similar to those that existed before British Rail was nationalised. Ultimately the decision was taken to separate the railway infrastructure from the provision of passenger and freight services with a new company, Railtrack, created to take over ownership and management of the infrastructure and larger stations; there are still some schools of thought that feel separating the infrastructure from train operators was a mistake.

Unlike the train operating companies who had to be successful in winning a franchise for the rights to operate services, the new company operated as a licensed custodian, in reality owning its assets in perpetuity provided it did not seriously breach its license conditions. Railtrack had taken control on 1 April 1994 but by 1999 the company was facing severe criticism on both its safety and maintenance procedures, not helped by fatal accidents at Southall (1997) and Ladbroke Grove (1999). The spiralling costs it faced over the West Coast Main Line upgrade together with the consequences of a further fatal accident at Hatfield in October 2000, left the company in serious debt. It was no surprise when, in early October 2001, Railtrack found itself in Railway Administration under the Railways Act 1993, where it remained for twelve months. The government had hoped that several private bidders would be attracted to make bids to take over Railtrack's role and must have been disappointed that this did not happen. Instead the newly formed Network Rail (NR), a non-profit company, took over Railtrack and its assets on 3 October 2002.

British Rail's passenger services were divided into twenty-five fixed-term franchises, as well as some extra ones for freight. To oversee the franchising programme a new government department, the Office of Passenger Rail Franchising (OPRAF), was created and given special responsibility for letting the new franchises. Today the Department for Transport has taken over responsibility from its predecessors, OPRAF and the Strategic Rail Authority, for running competitions for the award of new franchises. After consulting with stakeholders and specifying the passenger rail services to be run as well as the operating standards such as punctuality and reliability which have to be met, the franchise is awarded to the bidder who offers the best and most robust proposition in terms of deliverability and price. After the franchise is awarded, the Department for Transport has the responsibility to monitor performance and ensure any failings are corrected. Failure to put things right can ultimately lead to withdrawal of the franchise. It was intended that franchise holders would eventually pay a premium to the government for the right to operate the services specified under the terms of the franchise agreements. Winning bidders were required to enter into a track access agreement with Railtrack, allowing them to use the infrastructure, and the government expected Railtrack to use this additional income to bring the infrastructure back to good order. Interestingly, the InterCity network had been operating 'in the black' under British Rail (BR) but the new access charges almost doubled the equivalent operating costs for the new franchise holders.

With TOCs having to pay additional leasing fees to rolling stock companies (ROSCOs), which had also passed into private ownership, plus staffing, station, and training costs, it quickly became obvious that many of them would require a subsidy from the government for some time before they would be able to pay the required premiums. Their only source of income was from the fare-box. Ironically, the total compensation paid out to the TOCs by OPRAF to cover this amounted to £1.6 million in 1994/95, which was some 58 per cent higher than the previous year—British Rail's last.

Opposite above: HST sets caught resting between turns at London Paddington station's Platforms 2, 3, and 4 respectively on 2 September 2011 will eventually go forward with services to Plymouth, Swansea, and Bristol Temple Meads. The power cars seen on the right of the picture are Nos. 43171 and 43158. (*John Balmforth*)

Opposite below: London Paddington looking very smart (as is the young lady in the foreground) on a warm September day in 2011. (*John Balmforth*)

2

First Great Western: The Story

First Great Western

Once the decision to privatise Britain's railways had been made it was necessary for services to continue operating under BR stewardship until the franchises were let. In the meantime BR had to continue managing the network, effectively operating twenty-five franchises separately until the dates of sale. It also had a duty to prevent any deterioration in operations whilst at the same time beginning preparations for the handover to the successful bidders.

Managers had obvious conflicts of interest from running the business whilst preparing it for sale, especially if they were part of a team involved in a management and employee buy-out (MBO) bid. The Great Western franchise was one of the first three to be let, alongside London Tilbury & Southend (LTS) and South West Trains (SWT), and was itself the result of a successful MBO bid led by Brian Scott, who had headed the Shadow Train Unit of British Rail in the lead up to privatisation.

The original franchise commenced on 4 February 1996 as one of the InterCity operators. It was awarded for a period of seven years, to be operated by Great Western Holdings. The holding company was part owned (24.5 per cent) by the Badgerline Bus Group, which itself merged with Grampian Regional Transport (GRT) and 3i Investors, both companies holding the same number of shares. The powerful bus company became FirstGroup plc and purchased the remaining shares from its partner for a sum of £105 million in 1998, at the same time changing the company name to First Great Western, now with Richard George at the helm. Many commentators felt that the early franchises had been sold off too cheaply, a view in some ways supported by what was seen as the highly achievable reduction in subsidy of £61 million at the start of the franchise to £27 million by the time the franchise contract was completed.

After a period which had seen Dr Mike Mitchell, Andy Cooper, Mike Carroll, Chris Kinchen-Smith, and Alison Forster occupying the Managing Director's seat, the company successfully won a bid to also operate the Thames Trains franchise in 2004. The first step towards creating the present-day First Great Western really began in 2003 when the Thames Trains franchise was approaching its end. First Great Western made an unsolicited proposal to the Strategic Rail Authority that the Thames Trains franchise should not be extended but should instead be merged with First Great Western. FirstGroup and Go-Ahead (holder of the Thames Trains franchise at that time) were asked to cost plans and subsequently the SRA preferred the FirstGroup proposal. First Great Western already had fast Class 180 Adelante trains in use on the Bristol–Cardiff–Cheltenham route, which were getting very busy and carrying more people than had been expected; the management decided they should be replaced by refurbished HSTs.

In the meantime, fourteen new five-car Class 180 Adelante 125-mph diesel units had been ordered for their fast acceleration, which was ideal now that the services on many routes were seeing additional stops inserted. The existing HST sets were not suitable for this role, nor had they ever been intended to be. The plan was for the new Adelantes to be moved to the Oxford–Cotswold services to replace the Turbo trains operating there, whilst returning some of those to Chiltern Railways where they came from originally, with the remainder being used to strengthen other FGW services. It all made sense because First Great Western already shared some services with its former rival, Thames Trains. Although both train operating companies were in competition concerning stopping patterns in the Thames Valley, a lucrative source of revenue, they had created a new joint service for the Swindon–Bristol–Oxford route. To make this possible, track access rights for both companies were pooled.

First Great Western Link (formerly Thames Trains)

At that time the newly won franchise of Thames Trains was not absorbed straight into the First Great Western franchise, instead it operated alongside as First Great Western Link (FGWL) for two years. The new franchise operated services as follows:

- Great Western Main Line (Local services between London Paddington and Didcot Parkway).
- Cherwell Valley route (Didcot Parkway–Oxford)
- Cotswold Line (Oxford–Hereford)
- North Downs Line (Reading–Redhill)
- Reading to Plymouth route (Reading–Bedwyn)
- Reading to Basingstoke Line (Reading–Basingstoke)
- Slough to Windsor and Eton Line (Slough–Windsor & Eton Central)
- Oxford to Bicester route (Oxford–Bicester Town)
- Marlow Branch Line (Maidenhead–Marlow)
- Henley Branch Line (Twyford–Henley-on-Thames)
- Greenford Branch Line (London Paddington–Greenford)

Thames Trains had also originally operated services to Stratford-upon-Avon and from Reading to Gatwick Airport, but after the franchise changes these were transferred to Chiltern Railways. An additional franchise commitment was for First Great Western Link to supplement the inherited thirty-six Class 165/1 Network Turbo and twenty-

A statue of Isambard Kingdom Brunel standing in its rightful place next to Paddington's Platform 1 reminds the thousands of people who pass it every day of the debt rail passengers owe to the founder of the Great Western Railway. (*John Balmforth*)

Night-time photographs of the railway are always pleasing on the eye and this one of a Class 180 Adelante at Paddington is no different. The train shed roof aided by the coloured lighting is worthy of note and matches the train's livery. (*John Balmforth*)

Class 166 Express Turbo Unit No. 166206 in First Great Western Link livery arrives at London Paddington on 25 August 2004 with a service from Oxford. Class 43 HST power car No. 43143 can be seen in the background. (*Brian Morrison*)

Trains in regular daily commuter use always suffer heavy signs of wear and tear, and this Class 165 Networker Turbo Unit is in desperate need of refurbishment. (*Courtesy of First Great Western Photo Archive*)

Compare this photograph with the previous one to see the improvement that came with the unit's refurbishment. (*Courtesy of First Great Western Photo Archive*)

three Class 166 Network Express Turbo trains, (both 90-mph units maintained at Reading DMU depot), with the transfer of five Class 180 Adelantes from First Great Western. This allowed the remaining units to be transferred to Chiltern Railways. After the changes, First Great Western Link did not operate any services north of Banbury.

Wessex Trains

Commencing in October 1996 as part of the South West & Wales franchise, and operating services as the name suggests in Wales and the West of England, the company also ran services to: Liverpool Lime Street, Manchester Piccadilly, Birmingham International, Southampton, Brighton, and London Waterloo.

In 2001 the Strategic Rail Authority had reorganised the Valley Lines and Wales & West franchises, both then operated by National Express. This transferred the Welsh services to Wales & Borders with the West of England services remaining with National Express and operating as Wessex Trains, who did retain some services to Cardiff.

The new Wessex Trains franchise operated services from Great Malvern & Cardiff to Brighton, Portsmouth, Weymouth, and Penzance, and also on the following routes:

- Atlantic Coast Line (Par–Newquay)
- Avocet Line (Exeter–Exmouth)
- Golden Valley Line (Swindon–Gloucester)
- Heart of Wessex Line (Westbury–Weymouth)
- Looe Valley Line (Liskeard–Looe)
- Maritime Line (Truro–Falmouth)
- Riviera Line (Exeter–Paignton)
- Severn Beach Line (Bristol–Avonmouth–Severn Beach)
- St Ives Bay Line (St Erth–St Ives)
- Tamar Valley Line (Plymouth–Gunnislake)
- Tarka Line (Exeter–Barnstaple)

It was originally planned for the Wessex franchise to include the diesel-hauled services operated by South West Trains between Exeter and London Waterloo, but this did not come to fruition. Rolling stock inherited with the franchise, to be serviced at either Cardiff Canton or Exeter Traction Maintenance/DMU depots, was:

	Top Speed mph/kph	No. of units
Class 143 Pacer	75/120	7
Class 150 Sprinter	75/120	25
Class 153 Super Sprinter	75/120	13
Class 158 Express Sprinter	90/145	12

On 7 March 2012, FGW Class 150/2 No. 150249 is seen waiting at Bristol Temple Meads ready to form a service along the branch line to Severn Beach. (*Alun J. Caddy*)

Class 143 No. 143603 Pacer DMU, wearing FGW local lines livery, is pictured on depot in October 2007, probably at St Phillips Marsh, Bristol T&RSMD. (*Courtesy of First Great Western Photo Archive*)

In FGW 'local lines' livery Class 150/2 No. 150244 approaches its Dawlish stop on 1 September 2007. (*Brian Morrison*)

One of FGW's Pacer units, No. 143603, is seen in 'local lines' livery coming off the depot at Exeter. Photographed from Platform 6 at Exeter St David's, the blind suggests it is about to go forward with a service to Penzance. (*Courtesy of First Great Western Photo Archive*)

Mark 2 carriages	100/160	5
Class 31 locomotive	80/128	1 Leased from Fragonset to haul mark 3 carriages

* Source: *http://en.wikipedia.org/wiki/Wessex_Trains Wessex Trains*

Then First Great Western's own franchise period was extended, initially to run to February 2006 and later to 31 March 2006. The extension also coincided with government plans to revise the franchise network and reduce the number of TOCs; in this instance three became one (the new FGW=FGW+FGWL+Wessex) because the formerly National Express-held Wessex Trains franchise was also included.

Staffing

The railway is a labour-intensive employer and an operator the size of First Great Western does require high numbers of staff, in this particular instance some 5,352 staff consisting of: 1,169 engineering staff; 1,158 drivers, 702 guards, and train managers; and 2,323 catering and station staff, customer services, headquarters staff, and others.

Mark Hopwood told me that he had worked for a number of train operating companies but he considered the staff at First Great Western to be the best he had seen. Perhaps that's the result of the company's investment in its staff. The financial investment in staff training had resulted in the company having some of the best training facilities amongst all of the UK's TOCs. Driver training is carried out at specialist centres in Bristol, Exeter, Reading, Plymouth, and Westbury, and there are other training facilities for non-driving staff at Newton Abbot (training suites), Paddington (customer services training centre which includes a mock-up buffet car), and Reading (customer services training centre).

I am grateful for the opportunity to experience a driver's eye view (properly arranged and supervised at all times) between Plymouth and Taunton; cab views are always special as can be seen from the following photographs:

Request to re-negotiate the franchise terms

Changes were also negotiated around the First Great Western subsidy profile, which had not predicted the increased levels of passenger growth. The huge growth meant that the potential which the additional rolling stock coming in from Thames Trains (FGWL) and later from the merger of the Wessex franchise would bring was not realised, giving the company some severe headaches as rolling stock shortages began to take their toll on performance.

When I interviewed Mark Hopwood, he revealed that there was a very difficult period at the start of the new First Great Western franchise because people had underestimated the challenge of bringing together the three businesses. He said that the biggest problem was sorting out train service performance and that the story behind

Plymouth Councillor Tudor Evans is seen at the controls of a FGW HST Simulator under the guidance of Driver Simulator Manager Brian Clarke. (*Courtesy of First Great Western Photo Archive*)

Seen at Platform 7 Plymouth, having arrived when forming a service from Penzance with Class 43 power car No. 43025 *The Institution of Railway Operators* leading, the train will go forward at 12:01 on 24 April 2013 to London Paddington. (*John Balmforth*)

Inside the cab of power car No. 43025 Plymouth driver Andy Stewart is seen at the controls. The author was delighted to travel with him as far as Taunton, supervised by Brian Payne, Driver Competence Manager FGW Plymouth. (*John Balmforth*)

This must be a contender for the best driver's eye view as Class 43 power car No. 43025 approaches Dawlish, Devon, on 24 April 2013. (*John Balmforth*)

A comparatively recent installation in the cabs of FGW's HSTs is the DAS (Driver's Advice System) which helps drivers maintain time and save fuel. Seen on the lower right of the picture it provides important and useful information but is not intended to replace a driver's own route knowledge. (*John Balmforth*)

that went back to root causes in understanding problems with inheritance, not having enough trains, needing more drivers and guards, as well as getting Network Rail to deliver a more reliable infrastructure. A key component of the winning bid was taking the maintenance of the Diesel Multiple Unit fleet away from the Arriva Trains Wales depot at Cardiff Canton and moving it to St Phillips Marsh, Bristol. Hopwood told me that in hindsight, not enough work was done in planning this, and the maintenance of the DMU fleet was a real problem resulting in a lot of train service cancellations and consequent service disruption; the move out of Canton was probably a mistake. Coupled with this was the fact that Network Rail was not delivering at the time either, so the net effect was very poor punctuality and reliability. The cancellations threshold in the franchise agreement was triggered and that led to a change in senior management, not only at First Great Western, but also in the Network Rail route management.

Over the following two years performance underwent a sharp dip but it was not all the fault of First Great Western, far from it. The TOC had to operate services on worn out infrastructure and with some of its trains approaching thirty years of age. To make things worse, passenger confidence was diminishing in the wake of four fatal accidents, three of them involving First Great Western high-speed trains, at Southall, Ladbroke

One of First Great Western's Class 150/2 DMUs No. 150246 is seen making a station stop at Kemble when forming a Cheltenham Spa service on 11 January 2013. (*Courtesy of First Great Western Photo Archive*)

Holidaymakers turn to watch a FGW HST set as it passes Dawlish on 13 June 2010 on its way to Penzance. Power cars No. 43086 (front) and 43053 (rear) provide the motive power. (*Courtesy of First Great Western Photo Archive*)

Class 150/1 DMU No. 150102 arrives at Camborne on 30 May 2012 with a service from Bristol Temple Meads to Penzance. (*Alun J. Caddy*)

FGW two-car Class 150/2 with connecting gangway No. 150222 is seen passing Fairwood Junction to the west of Westbury on 24 April 2013. The unit is carrying local lines livery and is forming a service to Weymouth. (*Courtesy of First Great Western Photo Archive*)

Grove (which also involved a Thames Trains DMU), and Upton Nervett level crossing. Failures of the HST train sets coupled with deteriorating track conditions and an annoying increase in Temporary Speed Restrictions (TSR) combined to see an increase in service cancellations. On top of this, the shortage of reliable rolling stock and the growth in passenger numbers was not only upsetting for passengers but had also been noticed by the Department for Transport (DfT). First Great Western and the DfT had already been in disagreement over how much additional rolling stock performance could be achieved through the franchise mergers, and performance had got so bad by February 2008 that the DfT issued a breach notice—the first step towards withdrawing a franchise. In doing so the Secretary of State for Transport said, 'First Great Western had fallen persistently short of customers' expectations and been unacceptable to both passengers and government'. A Remedial Plan Notice was issued as a result of exceptionally high levels of service cancellations and low passenger satisfaction. Part of the plan required First Great Western:

- to achieve improvement milestones
- to lease five more Class 150 Diesel Multiple Units allowing three-car trains to be used on the Portsmouth–Cardiff route
- to undertake a much more extensive refurbishment of the Thames Turbo fleet

A FGW Class 150/1 two-car DMU is seen standing at Plymouth on 26 January 2012 waiting to form a service to Penzance. This is one of the units transferred from the West Midlands and is still wearing the green livery of an earlier operator, Central Trains. (*John Balmforth*)

A Swansea–London Paddington HST passes Slough at speed on 25 August 2004, led by Class 43 power car No. 43108 *The Red Cross*. (*Brian Morrison*)

- to offer 50 per cent higher compensation for the duration of the franchise
- to offer 500,000 more cheap tickets on off-peak services
- to improve station customer information systems.

Failure to meet the DfT's requirements would almost certainly have resulted in First Great Western losing its franchise. It didn't take long before the press, media, and passengers coined the nickname 'Worst Great Western' for the company; just a month earlier some passengers had launched a fares strike in the Bristol area, where customers suffering the withdrawal of some rolling stock found it impossible to even board trains because they were already 'full and standing'. Protesters went as far as producing an imitation ticket showing class of travel—'cattle truck', ticket price—'up 12%', and route—'to hell and back'. It was no surprise when the issue was featured on national television, revealing that several of the West Country branch lines were having trains replaced by bus services, albeit with the intention of this being on a temporary basis. On 22 December 2006, the First Great Western InterCity services were shown to be the worst in the UK for delays according to figures released by the Office of Rail Regulation. This led to First Great Western admitting that the anticipated increase in rolling stock productivity from the franchise merger with First Great Western Link and Wessex Trains had failed to materialise and that performance was not up to the company's own required standards. Quite simply, there were not enough trains in the fleet to cope with the growth in passenger numbers.

In October 2008, an article in *The Guardian* by Dan Milmo and Rob Evans examined the problems faced by First Great Western.

First Great Western was one of Britain's most overcrowded rail franchises and had warned ministers that it did not have enough services to cope with demand. In a warning that the government has put too much strain on the rail network, the operator has asked to renegotiate the terms of its £1.1 billion contract. It wants to reduce payments so it can buy more carriages and has warned it is overspending in order to accommodate customers.

Using the Freedom of Information Act the article revealed that FGW had requested a review of its contract because, under current terms, it does not run enough services in the West of England. In a presentation to the then Rail Minister, Tom Harris, FGW said the Department for Transport had put 'substantial service cuts' into the franchise when it was reviewed in 2006.

First Great Western is the only franchise to have been specified with substantial service level cuts—when will it be the right time to review it? FGW added that timetable cuts on the new CrossCountry franchise, operated by Arriva, were putting pressure on its own services and that South West Trains was leaving 'substantial gaps' in the West Country by withdrawing trains.

FGW and its parent, FirstGroup, nearly lost the franchise that year after breaching its franchise twice. The DfT found that First Great Western misled passengers by under-reporting service cancellations last year. It then broke the contract for a second time by exceeding the threshold for cancelled trains in the second half of 2007 because of staff

A westbound FGW HST service, headed by Class 43 power car No. 43041, is seen running into Platform 4 at Exeter St David's on 26 January 2012 with a large number of passengers awaiting its arrival. In the background standing at Platform 2 is a Class 143 Pacer unit waiting to form a service to Exmouth. (*John Balmforth*)

FGW Class 158/9 No. 158959 makes its scheduled stop at Southampton Central when forming a Cardiff Central to Portsmouth Harbour service on 3 April 2009. (*John Balmforth*)

shortages. The then Transport Secretary, Ruth Kelly, imposed a 'remedial agreement' that cost the franchise holder £29 million and forced it to buy more carriages, increase compensation payments to passengers and hire more staff.

The head of the rail passenger watchdog said the presentation to Harris underlined that the government had been too prescriptive in setting franchise terms that slashed services while demanding ever-higher premium payments. 'The railways are having their own liquidity crisis. They don't have enough trains, and carriages are the industry's currency,' said Anthony Smith, chief executive of Passenger Focus. He added 'In the future, franchises should take on a much greater level of passenger input.'

The DfT has rejected accusations that it is demanding too much from the rail network in exchange for too little investment. In fact it spent more than £1 billion on 1,300 new carriages to operate on the most overcrowded routes in the UK by 2014. Government investment in the rail network will fall over the next five years, with passengers making up the difference by footing three-quarters of the cost at about £9 billion a year.

First Great Western carries seventy-nine million passengers a year and operates services between London and Cardiff as well services in the West Country and the busy commuter routes in the Thames Valley. Its reputation reached a nadir in 2006 when passengers staged a one-day 'fare strike' in Bristol in protest over carriage shortages and timetable problems. However, FGW has since undergone a substantial management revamp and is running a more reliable service with nine out of ten trains arriving on time. A First Great Western spokesperson said: 'We meet regularly with the DfT and continue to discuss options to improve services.'

In fairness, whilst the facts contained in the article cannot be disputed, it should be understood that First Great Western's new management team was already well aware of the difficulties it faced and had begun the process of putting things right.

3

Fighting Back:
The Road to Recovery

First Great Western looked in depth at the problems and came up with an improvement plan which firstly was aimed at improving relations with Network Rail, ensuring the two worked together to identify problem areas of reliability, and secondly to recruit 200 new drivers and guards. On top of this, extra vehicles were purchased. The entire package cost the company some £29 million, enabling them to reduce the numbers of passengers who were unable to find a seat and improve reliability and punctuality. This enabled the company to invest in and secure the purchase of forty-eight additional carriages which entered service in February and September 2012. These were in addition to six carriages obtained for Bristol area services, creating 900 additional seats, and thirty carriages secured in the previous year for service in the West Country. Managing Director Mark Hopwood stated:

> We've seen an ever increasing demand for travel on our services. While that is gratifying in one respect, it can lead to overcrowding on peak services which is why we've been working for some time to secure additional carriages. We have worked hard to put together an innovative deal that really maximises the benefit to customers from the rolling stock currently available. This investment, some £29 million, will deliver thousands of extra seats for customers across our network.

The additional vehicles (announced by the Department for Transport in late 2011) provided another 924 seats into and out of Bristol in the morning and evening peaks, including 336 through Bath. One of the new carriages was put into service on the Truro to Falmouth line, allowing all services on the route to run as two-car trains. All in all this added a total of 2,100 seats over the day and doubled capacity on key services, including the very busy 0747 Falmouth–Truro. A further vehicle was used to strengthen services between Paignton, Exmouth, Exeter, and Barnstaple. In doing so a further 270 seats were provided through the morning and evening peaks, alleviating capacity issues affecting school children and commuters, most notably on the 15:54 and 16:55 services from Paignton. First Great Western also leased five new Class 180 Adelante units which replaced most of the Turbo DMUs on the North Cotswolds line between Worcester and London Paddington.

Additionally, First Great Western invested a further £29 million to deliver some customer service training—'Putting Customers First'—plus enhanced fares discounts. These were significant sums; recognising the improvements, the Department for Transport withdrew the remedial notice in June 2009. Equally important was the transformation in the company's performance, which by then had reached 94.6 per cent of trains arriving on time. Over the next two years, FGW became the best performing long-distance train operator—an achievement which should not be underestimated.

The measure of the company's recovery is reflected in its winning the Rail Operator of the Year award in 2010 at the Rail Business Awards, followed by being named the Customer Communication and Service Excellence winner just two years later, again at the Rail Business Awards. Recognition continued when, in October 2013, First Great Western's work to secure additional carriages and upgrade others for the London and Thames Valley services was recognised by the Chartered Institute of Logistics and Transport (CILT) at its Annual Excellence Awards, held in London.

FGW won the Passenger Transport Best Practice Award for the project, which had seen the forty-eight additional carriages mentioned earlier come into service across the company's network, creating 4,500 additional seats a day and boosting peak-time capacity in key areas by up to 10 per cent. As part of the project, FGW secured a Department for Transport agreement for the forty-eight additional carriages through the procurement of Class 180 Adelante trains, which needed upgrading, as well as Class 150 DMUs. HST services were also expanded by converting fifteen disused HST buffet cars into eighty-four-seat standard-class carriages. Speaking after the award, Mark Hopwood said:

> I would like to offer my thanks and congratulations to all our colleagues involved in this project. The work has already had a significant impact on improving customers' journeys and reducing crowding, but now it is being recognised across the industry. In 2010, all of the top ten busiest trains into London were ours. Because of this, and other work around the business, we've reduced that to just one First Great Western service. Of course we need to do more, and the new franchise awarded earlier this month will help us do that. Already we have increased standard capacity on some of our Turbo commuter trains in the Thames Valley by 27 per cent by removing some First Class areas, and discussions with the Department for Transport are underway to talk about how we can do the same on our long distance services. Crowding and punctuality is of key importance to our passengers. Achieving recognition for being innovative in our industry, responding to customer needs, is a great honour.

He was absolutely correct because, just a couple of years earlier, First Great Western had been shown to be the operator carrying the most passengers in excess of capacity in the South West region; it was reported to have held the record for the most overcrowded train when one of its services carried almost double its intended capacity.

All train operating companies have performance and financial targets built into their franchises, and as we have seen, First Great Western had, in the past certainly, been failing to meet a number of these. TOCs are measured by a Public Performance Measure

Class 57/6 locomotive No. 57602 and Class 43 HST power car No. 43141 are seen at London Paddington on 6 May 2004. (*Brian Morrison*)

A line up of HST power cars, a Class 180 Adelante and a Class 332 Heathrow Express are seen at London Paddington's buffer stops on 16 May 2005. (*Brian Morrison*)

Passengers will be enjoying the sea view as Class 43's Nos. 43198 and 43085 provide the power for a service to London Paddington as the train passes Langstone Rock, Dawlish, when travelling along the scenic sea wall on 13 June 2010. (*Courtesy of First Great Western Photo Archive*)

Class 175 Coradia DMU No. 175115 departs Newport on Bank Holiday Monday 30 May 2005 forming a service from Cardiff Central. (*Brian Morrison*)

(PPM) and Moving Annual Average (MAA) score and these show that the changes made following Mark Hopwood joining the company had resulted in considerable improvements. There are set targets for both PPM and MAA which if triggered, require partial refunds to be made for the holders of season tickets valid for one month or more. The tables below give a snapshot of this as it affects First Great Western:

Performance results for 23 June–20 July 2013

	Punctuality per cent	Punctuality Target per cent	Reliability per cent	Reliability Target per cent
High-speed services	86.3	90.0	99.3	99.2
London–Thames Valley services	86.5	92.0	98.9	99.0
Bristol Suburban services	87.9	92.0	99.3	99.5
Devon services	93.9	92.0	99.2	99.5
Plymouth & Cornwall services	97.4	92.0	99.3	99.5
South Wales–South Coast services	89.7	92.0	99.2	99.5

* Source: First Great Western.

Twelve months Moving Annual Average from 22 July 2012

	Punctuality per cent MAA	Trigger per cent	Reliability per cent MAA	Trigger per cent
High-speed services	87.4	88.0	99.2	98.2
London–Thames Valley services	85.7	89.0	98.8	98.0
Bristol Suburban services	90.8	89.0	99.1	98.5
Devon services	95.4	89.0	99.5	98.5
Plymouth & Cornwall services	98.0	89.0	99.3	98.5
South Wales–South Coast services	92.5	89.0	99.2	98.5

* Source: First Great Western.

First Great Western still faced major challenges from an ageing infrastructure and the knock-on effect from temporary speed restrictions, but a closer working relationship with Network Rail began overcoming many of the recurring infrastructure problems. It can be seen in both tables that FGW failed to reach the target figures in some areas, but the company is delighted that it did meet all of the performance challenges that were under its own control.

During December 2005, it had been announced that First Great Western was the successful bidder, being preferred to National Express and Stagecoach, for the right to operate the new 'Greater Western' franchise which it would continue to operate using the First Great Western brand name for up to ten years, initially for a seven-year period, with a three-year extension available provided certain franchise commitments were achieved. When the new franchise commenced, First Great Western was in receipt of government subsidy but over the life of the franchise it was expected to pay over £1.13 billion in premium payments, some £313 million falling due during the final twelve months. First Great Western did not take up the option of the three-year franchise extension and some commentators, perhaps a little unfairly, suggested the company was pulling out early to avoid the high premium payments it would have to make. When I asked Hopwood about this, he replied as follows:

> That wasn't true and there were two main reasons why the option to extend the franchise had not been taken up:
> * The original agreement had been written in 2005 taking into account things like the Reading station improvements and InterCity Express (IEP) programme. With the way it turned out First Great Western felt it better to have a new agreement rather than to try to manage its way through an agreement that was never really written to properly take those things into account.
> * Commercially it just didn't stack up and at the end of the day it was an option for us to exercise if we wished.

Some people have tried, rather unhelpfully, to compare the First Great Western franchise to the Great North Eastern Railway (GNER) and National Express East Coast (NEEC) franchises, both of which failed. Hopwood said:

> All sorts of language was used but we've [FGW] never thrown in the keys, never walked away from the franchise and never refused to honour our obligations. Yes there was an opportunity for us to run the business for another three years but it was entirely optional and it was our decision not to. At the end of the day we've taken the same decision that any sane commercial undertaking would have done about running it for a further three years in an environment that was completely different to when the franchise was negotiated and in a way that would have resulted in us losing money for our owner. That was clearly not sensible and I don't think any other business would have chosen to run it either.

Hopwood's reasoning is sound but some people were quick to point out that in taking that action, First Great Western avoided paying £826.6 million to the government in premiums. They may have been correct but no business can realistically continue to trade knowing it is making a loss.

The franchise changes meant that First Great Western would continue to operate the long-distance main line services between London Paddington, the West of England, Bristol, South Wales, and the Cotswolds as well as the Night Riviera sleeper service to Penzance. The London suburban services previously operated by First Great Western Link (Thames Trains) were, of course, now formally incorporated into the new franchise alongside regional routes and branch lines that had been operated by Wessex Trains, which had been part of the National Express Group. Integrating the three franchises into one was not easy and was also a factor in the declining performance previously mentioned, not of course helped by the frequency of changes at the top of the company which had nine managing directors in twelve years. The measure of this is illustrated in Appendix A, in which the managing directors are shown alongside the company timeline.

There was an additional franchise requirement to reduce the train fleet at a time of heavy growth in passenger numbers, which proved impossible to achieve and led to the disagreement with the Department for Transport over the amount of rolling stock that could be saved by the franchise mergers.

With Andrew Haines now at the helm and Mark Hopwood appointed as Performance Director, First Great Western began the fight back. Despite the recession, the Thames Valley and West of England lie in some of the more prosperous areas of the country and passenger volumes continued to grow, so First Great Western had to find a way of bringing in extra vehicles. Hopwood pointed out that if he went back to the bare bones of the franchise agreement signed in 2005, the company would have had to operate the whole of the former Wessex franchise with 102 vehicles. That fleet has now been increased to 161 vehicles. He felt, and he was right, that this showed just how far the company had moved forward, adding that they had worked closely with the Department for Transport, other TOCs, and local authorities, to put together the package that resulted in the extra vehicles entering the fleet. In fact as Class 172s arrived at the London Overground and London Midland franchises, First Great Western was able to take all of London Overground's Class 150 DMUs and most of London Midland's. In addition to these, a pair of Class 153 single-car diesel multiple units, sometimes called railcars, were taken from London Midland, and the five off-fleet Class 180 Adelante units were returned to service for use on the Thames Valley routes. He said they didn't just look at obvious solutions, but also converted some off-fleet buffet cars, stripping them out and turning them into conventional trailer cars. FGW revealed that there had been no real opposition from passengers to this because there was still a buffet car in every HST set.

Hopwood eventually became Managing Director himself in 2008 and arrived on the back of almost twenty years of railway experience. He joined British Rail's Western Region in June 1989 and returned there after university, before moving on to employment with Thames Trains where he remained until 1999. This was followed with time at First North Western, Network Rail, and National Express in London, before returning to his original railway roots with First Great Western. His appointment finally brought stability at the top, ending the merry-go-round of occupants of the top position. Hopwood is still in the post at the time of writing, and without doubt this has been a major reason for the improvement in First Great Western's performance.

Hopwood's in-depth knowledge of the rail industry soon produced benefits. The supply of forty-five extra vehicles above the 102 previously written into the franchise, together with additional stops at stations including Slough and Maidenhead, inserted into some long distance services during the peak periods, resulted in an immediate improvement to Thames Valley commuter services. There would soon be the completion

FGW Class 158/9 DMU No. 158952 is caught by the camera near Frome on 24 November 2013. (*Courtesy of First Great Western Photo Archive*)

An HST set powers its way along the famous sea wall when forming a London Paddington bound service just after passing non-stop through Dawlish on 16 June 2008. Only the lady in the brown top, who may have just photographed the train, is giving it any attention as it passes with power car No. 43191 leading the way. (*Courtesy of First Great Western Photo Archive*)

A service for Bristol Temple Meads departs from London Paddington on 16 May 2005 with HST power car No. 43024 on the rear. (*Brian Morrison*)

Unusually for an HST set, this train is formed of the two power cars and just three coaches. It is seen crossing Brunel's famous Tamar Bridge heading into Cornwall on 3 April 2006, soon after the new FGW franchise commenced. The toll road bridge linking Devon with Cornwall can be seen in the background. (*Courtesy of First Great Western Photo Archive*)

of a total refurbishment of the HST fleet, bringing an end to the unacceptable number of failures and associated service cancellations. Prior to 2008, First Great Western had generally been at the bottom of performance tables (and it did not matter which table was looked at), but over the next two and a half years, the operator steadily climbed them. By 2010, with PPM reaching a healthy 92 per cent, the company now found itself at the top of the table, with its proud Managing Director revealing that cancellations had virtually been eliminated.

Record Breaking Cardiff to London non-stop train

The improvements were celebrated when on 26 October 2011 the Welsh Secretary, Cheryl Gillan, joined business leaders and other dignitaries on board a special First Great Western non-stop journey between Cardiff and London Paddington. The journey was an attempt to beat the then current fastest record of ninety-seven minutes and thirty-seven seconds, set in August 1988. The idea was to give a glimpse of the future when electrification should easily reduce journey times between the two cities to under two hours, and thus demonstrate the benefits and future investment possibilities to the business community. Gillan said:

> I am delighted to be on board First Great Western's non-stop journey from Cardiff to London today. This special train shows how well connected South Wales is to London and just what a short journey it is between the two Capital cities.

In response, Mark Hopwood commented:

> First Great Western prides itself on innovation and thinking about what we can do to improve services for our customers. This is an ambitious record attempt but win or lose it will be great to be able to demonstrate the possibilities for future Cardiff to London travel. South Wales is a very important market for us and around a third of our high-speed services service the country. It is not only a significant business hub, but also a fantastic cultural and tourism centre, and we recognise the importance of rail travel to those industries and the wider community.

Ambitious the attempt may have been, the train set a new record time of ninety-six minutes nineteen seconds.

The First Great Western franchise was due to expire in October 2013 and four major UK train operators, which had expressed an interest in operating the replacement franchise, each received an Invitation to Tender (ITT). These were First Great Western Trains Ltd (FirstGroup plc), GW Trains Investments Ltd (Arriva UK Trains Limited/DB (UK)), NXGW Trains Limited (National Express Group plc), and Stagecoach Great Western Trains Ltd (Stagecoach Group plc).

With the winner due to be announced in March 2013, the new franchise would run until July 2028, including an option for the Department for Transport to extend it

Seen travelling at speed through the countryside on 12 June 2007 is one of FGW's high-speed trains. (*Courtesy of First Great Western Photo Archive*)

FGW three-car Class 158/9 DMU No. 158956 is seen passing South West Train's Northam Depot, Southampton, while forming a Cardiff Central–Portsmouth Harbour service on 24 April 2009. (*John Balmforth*)

Her Majesty Queen Elizabeth II travelled to Penzance on the Royal Train *en route* to the Isles of Scilly where she opened a sports hall on 3 June 2011. She was met at Penzance by Prince Phillip who had travelled down by helicopter; after greeting people at the station, they continued their journey by helicopter. (*Courtesy of First Great Western Photo Archive*)

To celebrate the Diamond Jubilee of Her Majesty Queen Elizabeth II a Class 43 power car received wrap-around vinyls. A very smart looking 43186 is seen at Plymouth ready to form the 07:02 service to Penzance on 3 May 2012. (*Courtesy of First Great Western Photo Archive*)

for seven reporting periods. Proposals announced on the government's own website (ww.gov.uk/ government/news) on 27 July 2012 by the then Rail Minister, the Rt. Hon. Theresa Villiers MP, showed that the new fifteen-year Great Western franchise would see passengers benefit from new express trains, additional capacity, smart card ticketing, and passenger satisfaction targets.

> The number of train services required by the new franchise will be based broadly on the current timetable, rather than the contracted minimum in the existing franchise. The popular sleeper service to Penzance will be retained. An extra early, fast train from London to Plymouth will be introduced. This will achieve aspirations for a 'there and back in a day' service to Plymouth from the capital. Successful extra local services such as those on the Truro to Falmouth, Par to Newquay and the Severn Beach lines, including those which are locally funded at present, are being added to the base specification of the franchise. This recognises the valuable work and track record of investment made by local stakeholders. Full responsibility for funding these local schemes is expected to pass to the Department for Transport from 2015, securing their future and freeing up local resources for other transport priorities.
>
> Passengers using the Great Western Main Line will benefit from major infrastructure improvements and new rolling stock over the next few years, as a result of the Government's ambitious programme of rail improvements, including electrification. For the first time in the Great Western franchise, we will be introducing requirements on passenger satisfaction for the Train Operator to meet, which will mean they have to focus strongly on the issues that matter most to passengers. Extending smart card ticketing across the franchise will provide many more passengers across the West and South West with the kind of convenience Oyster has brought to Londoners. This new franchise will see additional capacity delivered to benefit passengers. A more efficient and flexible franchise will encourage private sector investment, for example in improving stations and rolling stock. It will promote greater efficiency and also enable the Train Operator to react more effectively to changing passenger demands.

The following table illustrates some of the options that the Invitation to Tender required:

Services to Cornwall	Continued operation of nine through services. Provision of a half-hourly regular service between Plymouth and Penzance or Exeter, from May 2017 when cascaded rolling stock is anticipated to become available.
Trans Wilts Rail (Phase 1)	Additional weekday rail services and reinstatement of Sunday services from Salisbury to Swindon via Melksham.
Riviera Line strengthening Exeter–Paignton	Introduction of an additional one train per hour service on the Riviera Line from Newton Abbot to Paignton.

Class 43 HST power car No. 43156 heads its train into St Erth while forming the 10:00 service from Penzance–London Paddington on 21 October 2011. The mixture of semaphore signals and thirty-year-old rolling stock is a reminder of the difficulties faced by First Great Western, at least as far as outdated infrastructure and elderly trains the franchise inherited go. (*Alun J. Caddy*)

Still equipped with semaphore signals, St Erth station is seen on 21 October 2011. The main line to London bears away to the right while the line to the left is the St Ives branch. Trains using the branch arrive and depart from the platform behind the metal fence and are controlled by the signal on the far left. (*Alun J. Caddy*)

Having arrived at Plymouth with a service from Penzance, Class 150/1 DMU No. 150106 is seen waiting to make the return trip on 26 January 2012. The unit was transferred to FGW from London Midland and still carries the previous Central Trains green livery. (*John Balmforth*)

Class 150/2 DMU No. 150248 is seen during the station stop at Bristol Temple Meads on 7 March 2012 when forming a Portsmouth Harbour to Cardiff Central service. The train carries FGW's 'local lines' livery. (*Alun J. Caddy*)

Arriving at Penzance station on 30 May 2012 is FGW Class 153 single car DMU No. 153373 coupled to an unidentified sister unit having completed the long journey from Exeter St David's. Not ideal for a journey of this length, they are better than no train at all. Nevertheless passengers would probably prefer to make the journey on the HST set seen in the background. (*Alun J. Caddy*)

Heart of Wessex Line Service optimisation	A much-strengthened service on the Heart of Wessex Line between Bristol and Weymouth.
Bristol Metro (Phase 1)	An advanced scheme developed by the West of England Partnership. Phase 1 will provide a half hourly service in the Greater Bristol Metropolitan area, including reopening of the rail line to Portishead to passenger services.
Devon Metro	Devon Metro follows a similar concept to Bristol Metro for local services but into Exeter, from Exmouth, Barnstaple, Newton Abbot, and Paignton. It also proposes additional new services on the South West Trains route to Okehampton.
Cornish Branch Line Service enhancements	St Ives trains extended to Penzance. Additional summer Monday–Saturday Looe Valley services.
Tavistock–Bere Alston re-opening	Re-opening of the rail line from Bere Alston to Tavistock.

* *Source: www.gov.uk/government/news/new-great-western-franchise*

Despite the amount of work involved, the costs in preparing franchise bids to satisfy the above, and the collapse of the process of re-letting the West Coast Main Line (WCML) franchise, which had initially been awarded to FGW's parent company FirstGroup, the Department for Transport extended a number of franchises for short periods without competition. The First Great Western franchise was amongst them. It was announced in September 2013 that the franchise would be extended by a new short-term franchise of twenty-three months until 2016 (the maximum allowed under EU regulations), leading to costly compensation claims against the government. When that expires it is expected that a similar short franchise extension will again be awarded by the Department for Transport. I would be surprised if First Great Western is not asked to be the operator, with the franchise then returning to open bidding in around 2018. An announcement on the FirstGroup plc website dated 31 January 2013 stated that 'the extension to 2016 would be used to ensure continuity of service and enable First Great Western to continue to deliver improvements for passengers throughout this longer period.'

4

Stations, Infrastructure and On-Board Services

Following a reduction in the number of UK rail franchises, the new Greater Western franchise (First Great Western) incorporated the previous Great Western InterCity, London & Thames Valley (Thames Trains), and West Country (Wessex) regional franchises. By December 2013 it was running 9,000+ services every week using more than 900 rolling stock vehicles. Of these, seventy new vehicles were introduced by FirstGroup prior to 2006, with a further one hundred by First Great Western since 2006, making a total increase of 23 per cent (source: FirstGroup website announcement, 28 July 2013). FGW was now operating more high-speed trains than at any time since the network was built, with increased frequencies including a half-hourly service to Cardiff and trains every fifteen minutes to Bristol. First Great Western is responsible for managing 208 stations and calls at a further sixty-eight stations managed by Network Rail or other train operating companies, carrying more than 90 million passengers a year. A total of 170 stations have car parking, providing in excess of 16,600 spaces. These range from three spaces at Portsmouth Arms to 1,140 at Bristol Parkway (1,620 are available at Reading although that station is managed by Network Rail). First Class lounges are provided at London Paddington and Cardiff Central. Initially there had also been a lounge at Bristol Temple Meads but since most of the trains starting there do so at half hourly intervals many passengers just got straight onto the train. Commenting on FGW stations, Mark Hopwood said:

> We spend large sums of our own, DfT and Network Rail money. It's a rash statement and I can't prove it but I'm willing to bet that we spent more on stations than any other franchise in 2012. Of course we have more stations than most and, of course, a huge investment by Network Rail at Reading.

As was promised by FGW, most station upgrade work was completed by the end of 2014. The list below, though not exhaustive, shows where the investment has been spent:

- West Drayton—platform extension work has been undertaken as part of CrossRail. This is also happening at many other FGW stations.
- Slough—large expenditure at this station has provided a new ticket hall, new ticket office, and new footbridge.

Seen on 2 September 2011, the entrance to London's Paddington station seems somewhat underwhelming. However, a quick glance to the right of the picture gives a glimpse of the magnificent roof. Only from the concourse and platforms can real justice be given to the roof design. Not seen from below in this picture, it is shown clearly in photographs reproduced earlier in this book. (*John Balmforth*)

The magnificent architecture of Cardiff Central station still bears the name of its early owner 'Great Western Railway'. The station is still extremely busy today with regular services provided by First Great Western, CrossCountry, and Arriva Trains Wales. (*Alun J. Caddy*)

The Great Western was noted for the beauty of many of its station buildings. In this case we see a glimpse of Bristol Temple Meads, which like Cardiff Central is still extremely busy with large numbers of passengers travelling to South Wales, the West of England, as well as the Midlands and the North East. (*Alun J. Caddy*)

The station building at Penzance does not have the grandeur of many of the big city Great Western stations but it is still of fitting design to mark the end of the line. It is the most south westerly station on the UK mainland; although it is possible to travel the short distance to Land's End by road, passengers wishing to travel further can only do so by air or sea. (*John Balmforth*)

With the running lines at Slough closed overnight for bridge replacement work, we see the new bridge between Platforms 2 and 3 being lifted into place in the early hours of 17 December 2011. (*Courtesy of First Great Western Photo Archive*)

- Maidenhead—the station has been completely refurbished.
- Twyford—a new footbridge and lifts have been installed.
- Newbury—a new ticket hall has been installed together with automatic ticket gates.
- Didcot—undergoing a rebuild at the time of writing (January, 2014).
- Swindon—a new forecourt and ticket gates have been provided.
- Cheltenham—new ticket gates installed.
- Gloucester—new ticket gates installed.
- Taunton—new ticket gates installed.
- St Austell—a new scheme was in the process of delivering a new footbridge at the time of writing (January, 2014).
- Truro—a new ticket hall and ticket gates installed.
- Exeter Central—rebuilt, including restoration of the London North Western Railway (LNWR) ticket hall, removing the need to use the little side entrance by going back to the traditional ticket hall, which British Rail moved out of in the 1970s.
- Bradford-on-Avon, Trowbridge and Westbury—£3 million spent on station improvements.
- Cotswold Line—double tracking installed.

Bath Spa

In February 2013 the First Great Western station at Bath Spa was awarded a red plaque by the Transport Trust in honour of Isambard Kingdom Brunel, acknowledging it as a place of significance and a point of focus on Brunel's Great Western Railway through the city.

Community Rail Lines

It is interesting to note that at the time of writing, First Great Western had six of the top ten community rail lines in the country. Speaking at the TravelWatch South West General Meeting in March 2013, Mark Hopwood announced that passenger numbers had reached two million for the first time on the Devon & Cornwall community rail lines, another record year.

These excellent results show the value of our local rail services in the South West and how productive partnerships can really deliver results that benefit local people and the local economy. Our local Community Rail services are not only among the fastest growing, but also among the most reliable in the country and we look forward to working with partners to deliver further improvements.

For the first time, all-year-round Sunday services had been introduced on the Atlantic Coast line to Newquay and First Great Western were rewarded with a huge 22.5 per

On a very overcast day in the West Country an unidentified Class 43 power car is seen at the rear of an HST set as it passes over a latticed girder bridge in Bath on 8 March 2012. (*Alun J. Caddy*)

cent growth in passenger numbers using the line. Passenger numbers on these branch lines has increased by 147 per cent since 2006—a quite remarkable figure. Last year the numbers for individual lines were:

- 500,000+   The Tarka Line
- 175,00+   The Tamar Valley Line
- 104,000+   The Looe Branch
- 84,000+   The Atlantic Coast Line
- 613,000+   The Maritime Line
- 500,000+   The St Ives Line

Services transferred to Chiltern Railways

A negative aspect of the franchise boundary changes for First Great Western was the Oxford–Bicester route being transferred to Chiltern Railways. Using its new chord, FGW admits that Chiltern will take some of its London market but does not think the loss will be that great as First Great Western still offers faster journey times and Paddington will be a better place to get into the new CrossRail route than Marylebone. Since First Great Western's business is growing so fast, equivalent numbers of those lost will be quickly regained and as such FGW do not see it as a significant issue.

Severe weather disruption

Snow and flooding are major issues for any railway and the UK's railways are no exception. Rules and regulations applicable to today's train operators are very different to those that applied back in the steam era of British Railways. It is now very rare for a train to be able to pass over an area of flooded track, and First Great Western faces this problem at a number of locations, including Cowley Bridge Junction, where the line to Barnstaple branches away from the main line north of Exeter. Mark Hopwood and his counterpart at Network Rail, Sir David Higgins, have met with ministers in parliament to discuss the problem. Hopwood revealed that the government recognises that something has to be done and not just on the railways. Often the simplest way to let water across the railway is to construct a bridge, but this requires government investment, as do better quality flood defences. When Cowley Bridge Junction is flooded, for example, it requires main line services including the sleeper trains to take a lengthy diversion via Yeovil, and services from Exeter–Barnstaple have to be replaced by buses. On the night of 27 October 2013, St Jude, the worst storm to hit the British Isles since 1987, caused major disruption and damage to the South and South West of England, with many train operators announcing there would be no trains before 0900 the next day. First Great Western services operate right across the regions hit by the storm, and like many operators was forced to cancel services in the interests of safety. The decision proved to be sound as the storm brought down many trees across the running lines, one of which resulted in a collision involving an empty stock HST *en*

Waiting at the platform of FGW's station in Barnstaple on 30 August 2011, ready to form a service to Exmouth, is Class 150/1 DMU No. 150123. (*Courtesy of First Great Western Photo Archive*)

Two-car Class 150/1 DMU No. 150101 is seen arriving at Bath Spa on 27 March 2013. The unit will continue as the 10:08 service to Great Malvern. (*Alun J. Caddy*)

Departing St Ives on 7 September 2011 forming a service to St Erth is Class 150/2 DMU No. 150266 coupled to an unidentifiable sister unit. Both units are wearing FGW 'local lines' livery. (*John Balmforth*)

One of FGW's two-car Class 150 DMUs leaves the beautiful sandy beaches of St Ives behind as it climbs towards Carbis Bay *en route* to St Erth on 14 April 2009. The unit is carrying FGW 'local lines' livery. (*Courtesy of First Great Western Photo Archive*)

Heavy snowfall is not something usually associated with Devon but on 21 December 2010 it fell in Exeter. Seen helping to clear the platforms at St David's station are Station Manager Stuart McClay (left), Driver Manager Brian Payne (right), and Lead Driver Fred Richards. In the background an HST set waits to continue its journey. (*Courtesy of First Great Western Photo Archive*)

FGW staff are pictured continuing to clear snow from the platforms on the same day. The unidentified HST set is probably heading for London. Meanwhile in the sidings can be seen a South West Trains Class 158 unit which is awaiting its return trip to Waterloo. (*Courtesy of First Great Western Photo Archive*)

route from Laira TRSMD to Paignton. In early 2014 exceptional storms struck again; this time severe damage was caused to the sea wall at Dawlish causing a 100 foot breach in the wall and for a time totally severing services between Exeter St David's and Cornwall. It is to the industry's credit that the wall was repaired in a relatively short time enabling services to recommence.

Reading Improvement Scheme

Although the responsibility of Network Rail, First Great Western's passengers will benefit enormously when the rebuilding of Reading station is completed. Services have had to operate through a huge building site whilst the work is carried out; some London to the West of England services temporarily departed from Waterloo instead of Paddington in order to accommodate the work. Obviously there has been some passenger disruption during the rebuild, but it cannot be denied that the impressive new station and the removal of a rail bottleneck will bring much required benefits to train operating companies and passengers alike. It has not been an easy operation to plan, and Network Rail, First Great Western, and the other TOCs using the station should be congratulated for working so closely together to bring about the much-needed improvements.

The upgrade of Reading station is part of the overall £850 million Reading Improvement Scheme. Whilst Network Rail will deliver the station and track upgrade (which began in 2010 and is due for completion in 2015, a full year ahead of schedule), Reading Borough Council will be making improvements to public spaces at the front and rear of the station. On completion, the station will provide more reliable services, ultra-modern facilities, and improved journeys from a station that will be equipped to deal with increased future passenger demand. Easter 2013 witnessed the completion of a major part of the upgrade for the benefit of passengers:

- A new passenger footbridge giving improved access to all platforms.
- Two additional entrances; one each at the north and south of the station.
- Four enhanced new platforms.
- More than 100 new customer information screens.

The remaining platforms are being refurbished and lengthened to accommodate longer trains.

A new and improved traction maintenance depot has replaced the old one and has been moved to the north side of the tracks, thus allowing for a new viaduct on the western approach to the station. The new viaduct, due for completion in spring 2015, will allow more room for trains and provide an alternative route for freight services, meaning fewer delays to passenger services entering or departing Reading.

There are on-going track and signalling improvements to promote smoother, more reliable train journeys, and the Over Head Line (OLE) structures, which will carry the power supply for the new state-of-the-art electric trains that will eventually serve Reading, are being put in place.

The station and infrastructure improvements at Reading have seen train operators running through what is effectively a large building site in order to maintain services. To reduce conflicting train movements after the upgrade, the DMU depot has been moved across to the other side of the tracks. It can be seen here as construction proceeds. (*Alun J. Caddy*)

The reconstruction of Reading station will provide excellent facilities for passengers. Here work is continuing with building new platforms. (*Alun J. Caddy*)

Electrification

Potentially the biggest disruption facing the winner of the next Greater Western franchise will be the Great Western Main Line electrification scheme. Work on the £1 billion project will be undertaken on the route of the existing line between Reading and Maidenhead in the east and Bristol in the west. It is due for completion in 2016, and then be extended to Cardiff by 2017. However, several services run beyond both Bristol and Cardiff to places such as Cheltenham Spa, Worcester, Hereford, Pembroke Dock, Weston-super-Mare, Exeter, Taunton, Plymouth, Penzance, and Swansea. These services would need to continue using diesel power which could be provided by new trains running in bio-mode, using both electric and diesel power. Such trains would need to take power from the overhead line power supply or on-board diesel generators. Many people in the Bristol area are concerned that the project could spell the end of through services between Weston-super-Mare and London, forcing commuters onto already crowded local services to Bristol. A campaign group supported by local MPs are lobbying for the electrification to be continued to Weston-super-Mare and also the Severn Beach Branch. A similar situation appeared likely in Swansea until it was announced in July 2012 that the route to the city would be included in the electrification programme; lines continuing to areas such as Carmarthen or Pembroke Dock are not to be included. The electrification programme will include spurs north to Oxford and south-west to Newbury. Electrification between Stockley Junction and Heathrow has already been undertaken and that from Stockley Junction to Maidenhead will be undertaken as part of the CrossRail project. Electricity supply will be from the National Grid.

First Great Western will be closely involved in improving rail services following completion of the electrification and InterCity Express projects, and whilst electrification will provide faster journeys and be much more environmentally friendly, it will undoubtedly cause some delays while the work is carried out, and not just to rail users; the 'pain today, jam tomorrow' element of the scheme will ultimately bring huge benefits. In a statement on its own website, Network Rail reveals that electric trains will have 20 per cent more seating when compared to diesel trains, provide quicker journey times because of superior braking systems, especially in urban areas where there are frequent stops, and are far quieter (in fact virtually silent when stopped at stations). It says electric trains also perform better than their diesel cousins and emit around 20-35 per cent less carbon, as well as having zero emissions at the point of use, helping to improve air quality in pollution hotspots such as city centres and main line stations. It is rightly claimed that electrification of the network will stimulate economic growth by better connecting towns and cities whilst at the same time creating jobs. The opportunity to offer more seats and more trains will definitely make it easier for people to travel to work and help open new opportunities for businesses. Electric trains are cheaper to operate than diesels, require less maintenance, and have lower energy costs; they are also lighter causing less damage to infrastructure, culminating in a more reliable railway.

In 2013, First Great Western had no new routes planned, although this may change when the requirements of the new two-year extended franchise are known. Although the HST sets will continue to provide the main long-distance services, Mark Hopwood,

Managing Director of FGW, would like to unlock the Thames Valley for the company, as well as the Gatwick Airport, Hereford, and Worcester services too. Additionally, he would like to see the provision of a bay platform in the middle of the Central Line at Greenford, and an extra two services a day to Brighton. He proudly pointed out that during recent heavy snowfall, First Great Western's services to Brighton still ran at a time when many other operators' trains were being cancelled. If successful in its bid for the next First Great Western long-term franchise, the company would also like to improve the West of England local services: Cardiff to Portsmouth and the Devon & Cornwall branch lines.

The Night Riviera sleeper service

First Great Western operates the Night Riviera sleeper train services between London Paddington and Penzance. The service is considered by the thousands of people who use it each year, both tourists and those travelling on business, to be a wonderful way of travelling to and from Devon and Cornwall. Having sampled the service when conducting research for this book, I can only concur.

Despite this, when the 2006 franchise was put out to tender there was a plan by the Strategic Rail Authority to withdraw the sleeper train. It considered the sleeper service to be poor value for money, even going as far as asking bidders for the new franchise to include cost options for its withdrawal. I find this suggestion very difficult to understand because it is a fairly popular service and today the train is nearly always fully booked, creating a profit for its operator. The SRA proposal caused considerable public anger and a campaign by Andrew Roden attracted support from several MPs; more than 7, 000 people signed a petition to save the service. Respected rail writer and historian Christian Wolmar described it as 'a testing ground for the ability of the department to push through cuts based on the sort of flimsy and dishonest evidence that resulted in so many cuts at the time of Beeching'. The campaign, which even gained support from the Governor of the Bank of England and other well-known personalities, was ultimately successful and the service was saved. I particularly like the comment made by Andrew Roden in *Rail 715*, in which he referred to passengers going to sleep in London and waking up in the blink of an eye in Penzance: 'London to Penzance in 15 minutes? Now *that's* high-speed rail,' he wrote.

The trains are hauled by a dedicated fleet of four named Class 57/6 Thunderbird locomotives (rebuilt from Class 47s), all named after castles in Devon or Cornwall:

- 57602 *Restormel Castle*
- 57603 *Tintagel Castle*
- 57604 *Pendennis Castle*
- 57605 *Totnes Castle*

The Night Riviera offers two types of sleeping accommodation—single or twin cabins—the latter utilising a bunk bed style, although the upper bed can be folded up if not in use. Berths are equipped with a duvet, wash basin, shaver point, towel,

Class 57/6 locomotive No. 57605 *Totnes Castle* is seen waiting to be coupled to the *Night Riviera* sleeper coaches at London's Paddington station platform 1 on 23 April 2013. It will depart as the 23:45 service to Penzance. (*John Balmforth*)

Sleeper carriage No. 10590 shows off the logo carried on all coaches of the *Night Riviera* at London Paddington on 23 April 2013. (*John Balmforth*)

A newly refurbished Mk3 sleeper carriage is pictured at Railcare, Wolverton (near Milton Keynes) prior to delivery to First Great Western. (*Courtesy of First Great Western Photo Archive*)

A VOLO TV coach is displayed at Paddington on 15 September 2005 taking its place as part of an HST set. (*Brian Morrison*)

The sleeping accommodation on board FGW's *Night Riviera* is very comfortable. In this view we see the twin-berth accommodation. (*John Balmforth*)

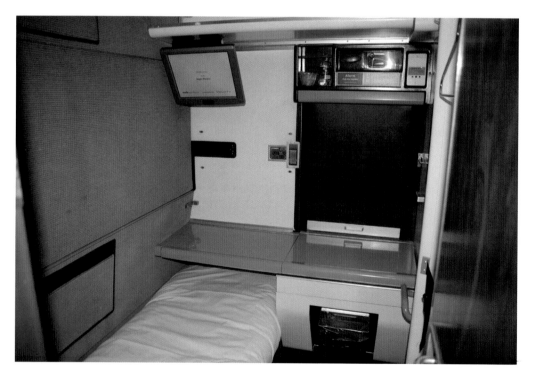

The *Night Riviera* single berths have VOLO TV fitted, unavailable in twin units because of the position of the upper berth. (*John Balmforth*)

Photographed on 23 April 2013 in Platform 1 at London Paddington is Class 57/6 Thunderbird No. 57602 Restormel Castle. The locomotive has just arrived with the *Night Riviera* sleeper coaches which will go forward hauled by *57605 Totnes Castle*. (*John Balmforth*)

bottled water, individually controlled lighting, and air conditioning. Additionally, the single-occupant cabins are fitted with VOLO TV, a free on-train video-on-demand service with a range of programmes. An interactive moving map facility is also included, providing real time information on the train's progress. The system was the first on-train entertainment system fitted to a fleet of trains in the UK. After a successful trial period in one of First Great Western's HST sets, it was installed on the Night Riviera sleeper service in early 2009, giving passengers a similar facility to that provided on airlines in First Class. In the same year, First Great Western won the award for 'Passenger Infotainment Innovation of the Year' at the prestigious Railway Interiors Expo in Cologne, Germany. Each train has four members of staff on board (excluding the driver): a train manager, a service leader, and two customer hosts, each responsible for one of the two sleeper carriages. Altogether FGW require twenty-one members of staff to provide the service. All (again excluding drivers) are based at Penzance except for train managers who are based at Exeter.

An extra benefit for passengers booked on the train is the use of the First Class Lounge at Paddington whilst awaiting departure time. Breakfast is provided free of charge and may be taken in cabins or the lounge car. Calling points for the train are: London Paddington, Reading (only on the westbound service), Taunton, Exeter St Davids, Newton Abbot, Plymouth, Liskeard, Bodmin Parkway, Lostwithiel, Par, St Austell, Truro, Redruth, Camborne, Hayle, St Erth, and Penzance.

The on-board lounge for holders of sleeper berth reservations on FGW's *Night Riviera* sleeper service. (*John Balmforth*)

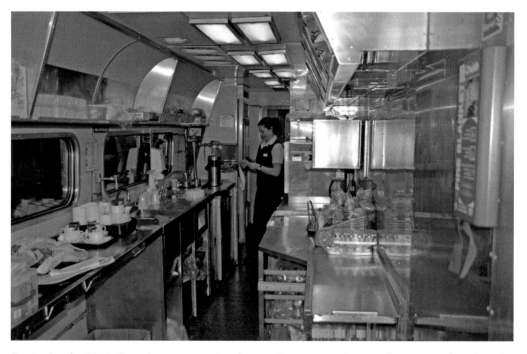

Service Leader Lizzie Dean is seen preparing the catering area in advance of passengers boarding the *Night Riviera* sleeper service on 23 April 2013. (*John Balmforth*)

FGW Customer Service hosts Alan Norton and Jade Winn are seen ready for the influx of passengers to the *Night Riviera* on 23 April 2013. (*John Balmforth*)

The Pullman Diner Service

A positive aspect of the franchise changes included a guaranteed continuation of the full Pullman Diner restaurant services on some trains. As the only train operating company in the UK that provides this facility, FGW decided to seek out a catering partner of exceptional passion and skill. Mitch Tonks, an award-winning restaurateur and chef, was that person, and he created a menu using fresh local produce, including sea food from the South West of England and Wales. The wine list was chosen from his own Seahorse restaurant in Dartmouth. In a message to passengers, he said:

> The menu is made up of dishes that I would eat on a journey, simple and full of pleasure and prepared and served by the great team on the Pullman services, it's a unique and quality dining experience. I hope you enjoy great eating, drinking and a wonderful journey.

Again having been fortunate enough to sample the product when carrying out my research, I must endorse Mitch's comments. It is a wonderful experience, made even more special by the uniforms of the waiting staff, which carry the Pullman emblem—a rather nice touch.

Food being served in the Pullman dining carriage by a highly trained waitress. Note the FGW version of the Pullman logo on her uniform. (*John Balmforth*)

The menu offered to customers using the FGW Pullman diner service. Designed for FGW by award winning Dartmouth-based chef Mitch Tonks, both the choice and quality of the food offered is excellent as can be vouched for by the author when he was invited to sample it on 24 April 2013. (*John Balmforth*)

Two of the Pullman diner main course dinners served up and ready to eat. On the left the choice was prime Somerset-reared fillet steak and on the right is Mushroom Wellington. (*John Balmforth*)

5

The Train Fleet:
Locomotives, Coaches,
Diesel Multiple Units, and Shunters

First Great Western operates a wide and varied fleet of trains, necessary because of its need to use fast high-speed trains as well as those more suited to stop-start local services. The Department for Transport franchise requirements issued in December 2008 enabled First Great Western to receive an additional fifty-two extra carriages in order to alleviate the serious problems the company was facing in the Bristol area. The DfT also indicated that an order for 202 new DMU vehicles would be made, but this never came to fruition. The order was cancelled after the announcement that the Great Western Main Line would be electrified. Instead the strengthening of First Great Western local services was to be facilitated by the cascade of existing diesel multiple units which would become redundant on completion of the electrification project. That is likely to bring yet another type of vehicle into the franchise if Class 319 units are transferred from the Thameslink route into Paddington. If this happens it will be possible to transfer the Class 165 Networker Turbo and Class 166 Networker Express Turbo units to local routes in the South West—a change which would be most welcome to passengers, but still some way off.

It is well known that the franchise will operate the new Hitachi Super Express trains resulting from the Intercity Express Programme (IEP) when electrification is completed, replacing the ageing (but much loved by passengers) HST sets. Nevertheless, it might not be the end of the HST as we know it today since they will still be required for services west of Bristol to Devon and Cornwall, which will not be upgraded by electrification in the immediate future. The electrification upgrade is much needed but the IEP Hitachi Super Expresses will need to serve routes which require both electric and diesel traction. Therefore, they may require the ability to operate in bi-mode diesel or electric traction, but even then it is unlikely that they will operate west of Plymouth.

During Alison Forster's time as Managing Director in 2005, work commenced on a substantial upgrade of the Class 43 HST fleet. The elderly power cars were fitted with new MTU power units, and at the same time their Mk3 carriages began a refurbishment programme. Those units intended for service in the M4/Thames Valley to Bristol, Cardiff, Exeter, Hereford, and Oxford were converted to a high-density layout of mostly airline-style seating with only two tables per carriage, enabling the provision of more seats for commuters. The remainder for use on routes to Swansea and the West

Looking across the train shed at London's Paddington station on 10 November 2011 reveals a line-up of five FGW high-speed trains as they take a breather between turns. Despite being around thirty years old, the sloping noses of these units still give them a reasonably modern shape and they are still popular with both passengers and staff. (*John Balmforth*)

Class 43 power car No. 43144 is seen approaching Swindon on 8 April 2013, heading the 13:28 HST service from Swansea to London Paddington. (*Alun J. Caddy*)

Seen in November 2013, FGW Class 165 No. 165218 is pictured at London Paddington's Platform 1 awaiting its next duty. Above the unit, the superb detail of the overall train shed roof can be seen clearly. (*Courtesy of First Great Western Photo Archive*)

Class 165/1 Networker Turbo Unit No. 165136 is seen departing Reading in November 2011 when forming a stopping service to Shalford. (*Courtesy of First Great Western Photo Archive*)

Country kept their original layout of tables at every seat. All of the refurbished coaches were fitted with leather seating in First Class and VOLO TV in some seat backs, usually in coach D.

The variety of rolling stock used by First Great Western is clearly illustrated below.

Class 08 Diesel-electric shunting locomotives

These powerful diesel locomotives were originally introduced by British Rail between 1953 and 1957 for heavy shunting duties; some 1,193 were manufactured by BR at its workshops in Crewe, Darlington, Derby, Doncaster, Horwich, and Landore. With a maximum permitted speed of only 15 mph (25 kph), appearances on the main line are rare, except at Penzance where they are used to ferry passenger coaches between the station and Long Rock TRSMD (PZ), but they are invaluable servants at traction maintenance depots. FGW has nine in service at the time of writing and like their more illustrious main line high-speed cousins they occasionally carry a nameplate; two of those presently in service with First Great Western receiving this honour are 08453 *Dusty-Driver David Miller* and 08645 *Mike Baggot*.

The ubiquitous workhorse, the Class 08 Diesel Shunter is found in the fleets of many TOCs. FGW's No. 08641 is pictured in the early hours of 24 April 2013 at Laira T&RSMD, resting between duties. The locomotive has a maximum speed of 15 mph but as can be seen by the information board above the buffer beam it is restricted to 5 mph on depot. (*John Balmforth*)

Class 43 high-speed train power cars

High-speed services for long-distance main line routes consist of pairs of Class 43 power cars interspersed by seven or eight Mk3 carriages providing a train capable of travelling at speeds up to 125 mph. The 196 power cars built between 1976 and 1982 have been described by some as 'the most successful high-speed trains powered by diesel locomotives anywhere in the world'. Originally built by BREL at its Crewe works, they can still be seen on almost all of the UK's main line network and since 2009 have been used on all FGW's long-distance services with the sole exception of the Night Riviera sleeper service.

First Great Western and Angel Trains conducted a trial in 2004 which involved two power cars being fitted with the powerful German MTU4000 16V power unit giving 2,700 hp (2,010kW), and two more receiving new MAN VP185s. The work was conducted at Brush Traction, Loughborough. The German MTU power unit proved to be better in both reliability and emissions, resulting in the original Paxman Valenta engines being replaced by the MTU power unit. The work was again carried out at Brush Traction, Loughborough; reliability is now good, bringing with it a high level of performance. A number of the power cars carry nameplates commemorating individuals including some former FGW employees, towns and cities, famous events, and military units, although this list is not exhaustive. At the time of writing the nameplates were as follows:

43003 *Isambard Kingdom Brunel*
43004 *First for the future/First ar gyfer y dyfodoi*
43009 *Transforming Travel*
43020 *MTU Power Passion Partnership*
43021 *David Austin* (cartoonist)
43024 *Great Western Society 1961–2011*
         Didcot Railway Centre
43025 *The Institution of Railway Operators*
43027 *Glorious Devon*
43030 *Christian Lewis Trust*
43033 *Driver Brian Cooper 15 June 1947–5 October 1989*
43037 *Penydarren*
43040 *Bristol St Phillips Marsh*
43053 *University of Worcester*
43056 *The Royal British Legion*
43070 *The Corps of Royal Electrical and Mechanical Engineers*
43087 *11 Explosive Ordnance Disposal Regiment Royal Logistic Corps*
43097 *Environment Agency*
43127 *Sir Peter Walker 1924–2002* (renamed *Cotswold Line 150*)
43132 *We Save The Children—Will You?*
43137 *Newton Abbot 150*
43139 *Driver Stan Martin 25 June–6 November 2004*

Class 43 power car No. 43004 *First for the Future / First ar gyfer y dyfodoi* at the head of the 13:25 service from Cardiff Central on 20 August 2012. (*Brian Morrison*)

This HST set headed by Class 43 power car No. 43127 *Sir Peter Parker 1974–2002 Cotswold Line 150* has arrived at Penzance after forming a service from London Paddington on 30 May 2012. (*Alun J. Caddy*)

An unidentified HST set is seen entering the west portal of Box tunnel on 3 November 2010 when forming a FGW Bristol Temple Meads to London Paddington service. (*Alun J. Caddy*)

On a heavily overcast and chilly day at the seaside on 4 September 2011, an HST is seen being readied to form a Penzance–London Paddington service. The leading power car is Class 43 No. 43033 *Driver Brian Cooper 15 June 1947 to 5 October 1999*. (*John Balmforth*)

First Great Western HST power car No. 43041 waits at Exeter St David's before continuing its westbound journey to Plymouth. Ahead of the set an unidentified Class 143 unit is seen branching off the main line to begin the steep climb to Exeter Central on its way to Exmouth. (*John Balmforth*)

Class 43 power car No. 43136 stands at Plymouth's Platform 4 at the head of its train ready to form a service to London Paddington. (*John Balmforth*)

First Great Western has continued the Great Western tradition of naming main line express locomotives. In this instance we see HST power car No. 43003 at Penzance carrying the nameplate of *Isambard Kingdom Brunel*, founder of the Great Western Railway, newly arrived from London Paddington. It will later form the 16:00 return service. (*Alun J. Caddy*)

43142 *Reading Panel Box 1965–2010*
43143 *Stroud 700*
43149 *University of Plymouth*
43156 *Dartington International Summer School*
43160 *Sir Moir Lockhead OBE*
43163 *Exeter Panel Box 21st Anniversary 2009*
43165 *Prince Michael of Kent*
43169 *The National Trust*
43175 *GWR 175th Anniversary*
43179 *Pride of Laira*
43185 *Great Western*
43189 *Railway Heritage Trust*
43198 *Oxfordshire 2007*

The majority of this class are owned by Porterbrook Leasing and Angel Trains although FirstGroup has purchased five sets outright.

High-Speed Train passenger carriages (Mk3)

Like the power cars which haul them, the HST passenger carriages inherited by First Great Western were almost thirty years old when the TOC won the franchise rights in 2006. They were of the Mk3 type, built originally for British Rail by Bombardier at its Derby works. Their spacious interiors had been an instant hit with passengers. The seating was comfortable and, unlike many modern designs of train, the vehicles had seating bays aligned with windows giving excellent views. Tables were also provided at every seat. Seating in standard class carriages was arranged four to a table in a 4x4 arrangement across the train, separated by a central aisle. In first class the seating was 2x1 across the vehicle with passengers benefitting from wider seats and extra leg room. When FGW upgraded its power cars the opportunity was also taken to refurbish the passenger vehicles; the work was shared between the Bombardier works in Derby, where they had been built so many years earlier, and Bombardier's premises at Ilford. Mindful of the need for extra capacity, FGW required extra seats to be fitted to each carriage, predominantly in the airline style. To do so required the vehicles to be completely stripped out and brand new interiors fitted. The additional seating was achieved but the airline-style seats installed in standard class had high seat backs which

The interior view of a FGW Mk3 HST standard class carriage after refurbishment seen in April 2008. (*Shirley Balmforth*)

Looking very smart after refurbishment is this first class Mk3 carriage from an HST set. Note the leather seats. (*Courtesy of First Great Western Photo Archive*)

When the HST Mk3 carriages were refurbished, a new design was created for the buffet cars to enable additional standard class seating to be installed. Despite the new café area being reduced in size it was still able to offer a reasonable array of refreshments for passengers. (*Courtesy of First Great Western Photo Archive*)

gave many passengers a feeling of claustrophobia. VOLO TV was fitted into the seat backs in many carriages and in first class leather seating was fitted, but continuing with the 2x1 seat arrangement.

The upgrade also included redesigned toilets, buffets, and at seat power points, and was completed by February 2008. Three HST units working on the London–Bristol–Cardiff & Exeter services had buffet cars removed to ascertain if improved performance could be achieved. However, no improvements were noted and the scheme was scrapped. FGW made the decision in the summer of 2008 that all of its HST sets should have buffet facilities but of a smaller design than previously used, allowing more standard-class seats to be installed. The new micro buffet had counters serving First Great Western's Express Café Menu. The upgraded vehicles were reclassified as Trailer Standard Micro Buffet (TSMB).

The majority of carriages being supplied for high-speed train services are leased from Porterbrook Leasing or Angel Trains, although as with the power cars FirstGroup has purchased a number of vehicles outright. The Mk3 carriages are allocated to Laira (LA) and Old Oak Common (OO) depots for maintenance purposes. Many years before privatisation, British Rail had introduced a coding system for its rolling stock called the Total Operations Processing System (TOPS), which allowed the location of every vehicle on the network to be identified. FGW's HST passenger vehicles were allocated TOPS classification codes as indicated in the following table:

Vehicle type	TOPS Code	Depot	Owner	Seating	Number of vehicles
Trailer Restaurant Standard Micro Buffet (TSRMB)	GN2G	Laira	Porterbrook	70 Standard	19
Trailer First Buffet (TRFB)	GN1G	Laira	Angel	23 First	6
Trailer Buffet (TRB)	GN1G	Laira	FirstGroup	23 First	5
Trailer First Buffet (TRFB)	GK1G	Laira Old Oak	Angel Angel	17 First 17 First	16 1
Trailer First Buffet (TRFB)	GL1G	Old Oak	Porterbrook	17 First	9
Trailer First (TF)	GH1G	Laira Old Oak Laira Old Oak	Angel Angel FirstGroup Porterbrook	48 First 48 First 48 First 48 First	41 34 10 22

Trailer Standard (TS)	GH2G	Laira	Angel	68-84 Std	88
		Old Oak	Porterbrook	68-84 Std	86
		Laira	FirstGroup	68-84 Std	21
		Old Oak	Porterbrook	68-84 Std	26
Trailer Guard Standard (TGS)	GJ2G	Laira	Angel	58 Standard	22
		Old Oak	Angel	58 Standard	19
		Laira	FirstGroup	58 Standard	6
		Old Oak	Porterbrook	58 Standard	11

Some carriages maintained by the Old Oak Common TMD (a specialist HST depot) are adorned with a logo based on the Pullman version on the carriage ends, complete with the words 'Old Oak Common HST depot'—a really nice touch.

Mk3 loco hauled and service (barrier) stock

In addition to its high-speed train passenger carriages, First Great Western also has the following locomotive-hauled vehicles in its fleet, which are mainly used for the sleeper service:

Mk3 loco hauled stock	TOPS	Depot	Owner	Seating	No. of Vehicles
Restaurant First Brake (RFB)	AJ1G	Long Rock, Penzance	Porterbrook	18 First	3
Sleeper (SLEP)	AV4G	Long Rock, Penzance	Porterbrook	12 sleeping compartments	10
Tourist Standard Open (TSO)	AC2G	Long Rock, Penzance	Porterbrook	45 Standard	2
Brake First Open (BFO)	AE1H	Long Rock, Penzance	Porterbrook	36 First	3
	Number				
Barrier Guard (BG)	6336 6338 6348	Laira	Angel	n/a	3
Barrier First (BFK)	6330	St Phillips Marsh	Angel	n/a	1

Seen on 24 April 2013, Laira's Class 08 Diesel Shunter No. 08641 is pictured hard at work shunting two Mk3 carriages from an HST set. The carriage nearest the locomotive carries the yellow stripe above the windows denoting that it is a first class carriage. (*John Balmforth*)

A specially designed badge appeared on the ends of some HST Mk3 carriages based at Old Oak Common HST depot. The enlarged inset shows off the badge to full effect. (*John Balmforth*)

Class 57/6 diesel locomotives

Originally built for British Rail by Brush between 1962 and 1964 as Class 47 diesel locomotives, which was then the largest class of diesel ever built, they were the second generation of main line diesel power in the UK. The class were seen all across the UK rail network working both passenger and freight duties. The Class 47 locomotives had been very reliable but their ageing Sulzer power units were now considered to be unsuitable for the work required of the locomotives; Porterbrook Leasing and Freightliner worked together on a project to find a low cost replacement.

In 2001 the Class 57/6 fleet of locotives was born using the body shells of the Class 47s they were replacing and fitted with General Motors 645-12E3 power units producing 2,500 hp (1,850 kW). First Great Western uses four members of the rebuilt class to haul its Night Riviera sleeper service and to act as Thunderbird rescue locomotives for failed HST sets. They are all named after castles:

> 57602 (previously 47337) *Restormel Castle*
> 57603 (previously 47349) *Tintagel Castle*
> 57604 (previously 47209) *Pendennis Castle*
> 57605 (previously 47206) *Totnes Castle*

In 2010, 57604 was repainted into Great Western Railway green for the 175th celebration at Didcot Railway Centre, the remainder wearing the corporate FGW blue livery. The entire Class 57/6 fleet was due to undergo refurbishment in January 2014, commencing with No. 57605 *Totnes Castle*.

Class 57/6 Thunderbird locomotive No. 57605 *Totnes Castle* is seen between duties on 25 March 2008. (*Courtesy of First Great Western Photo Archive*)

Class 142 Pacer Diesel Multiple Units

These train sets built between 1985 and 1987 consisted of Leyland Bus bodies attached to BREL underframes and were assembled at the BREL works, Derby. They operate in the formation of DMS+DMSL.

They provided between 103 and 122 standard class seats depending upon the vehicle's internal layouts. The trains became the largest fleet of 'Railbus' vehicles designed for use by British Rail on branch line services and operated mainly in the London Midland, Eastern, and Western regions of BR. The trains are fitted with one Cummins LTA10-R engine per vehicle, giving 460 hp (343 kW) per train and a maximum speed of 75 mph (121 kph).

First Great Western inherited seven of these units allocated to Exeter (EX) DMU depot; they were usually seen working the branch lines to Barnstaple, Exeter, and Paignton. It is fair to say that the Class 142 Pacer sets were disliked by staff and passengers alike, mainly because of the uncomfortable ride and Spartan interiors. They carried Northern Rails blue with gold star colours and never wore the new franchise holder's own livery. All had been transferred to Northern Rail by 2012.

Class 143 Pacer Diesel Multiple Units

Intended for service on local lines, these two-car DMU Pacer units delivered to British Rail were assembled in Kilmarnock at the works of Andrew Barclay using bodies supplied by bus manufacturer Walter Alexander on frames built by Hunslet in Leeds. Originally constructed between 1985 and 1986 they had one Cummins LTA10-R engine per vehicle providing 230 hp (171 kW) and a maximum speed of 75 mph (121 kph). First Great Western has eight units in service, all allocated to Exeter (EX) DMU depot. Leased from Porterbrook Leasing, they operate in the formation of DMS+DMSL.

With ninety-two standard class seats provided, they were usually found performing duty on the branch lines of Devon & Cornwall.

Class 150/0 Sprinter Diesel Multiple Units

These three-car units were built at BREL, York, in 1984 and work in a formation of DMSL+MS+DMS. Only two units of this class were built, nowadays carrying fleet numbers 150001 and 150002, and are fitted with one Cummins NT855R4 power unit per vehicle, giving 285 hp (211 kW) and a maximum speed of 75 mph (121 kph). They were prototype sets constructed when BR was looking for a new generation of trains to replace its ageing mid-distance DMU stock; the BREL design was chosen over a Metro-Cammell version. The two units operated by FGW were cascaded down from service with London Midland after that operator received its order for Class 172 DMUs and provided 240 standard class seats per train. Leased from Angel Trains, they have now been repainted in full FGW livery after operating for a brief period in their old Centro/Central Trains green colours.

Class 142 No. 142068 waits at Exeter St David's on 15 October 2007 ready to form the 09:56 service to Paignton. This was one of the seven units inherited by FGW and which never received the new operator's livery. (*Courtesy of First Great Western Photo Archive*)

Allocated to Exeter DMU depot, Class 143 Pacer No. 143603 is seen standing at the buffer stops on 15 October 2007. (*Courtesy of First Great Western Photo Archive*)

Class 150/1 Sprinter diesel multiple units

Built for BR at BREL York between 1985 and 1986, this class appeared as both two-car and three-car sets (the latter eventually being re-classified 150/9). Fitted with one Cummins NT855R5 of 285 hp (211 kW) per vehicle, the units had a maximum speed of 75 mph (121 kph) and can be seen throughout England and Wales in formations of two-car sets DMSL+DMS and three-car sets DMSL+MS+DMS.

FGW received fifteen of the class cascaded from London Midland and London Overground for use on the Bristol area commuter services, although today they are seen as far away as Plymouth and Penzance after the donors both took delivery of Class 172 Turbostars. This enabled FGW to return all of the Class 142 Pacer DMUs to Northern Rail and use the Class 143 units on the Devon and Cornwall local services instead. Pressed into service quickly, some units also served Penzance still wearing their previous user's livery, although they too would subsequently receive First Great Western's corporate livery. The units are leased from ROSCO Porterbrook Leasing.

Three of the class carried names:

150125 *The Heart of Wessex Line*
150129 *Devon & Cornwall Rail Partnership*
150130 *Severnside Community Rail Partnership*

Class 150/2 Sprinter diesel multiple units

Like their Class 150/1 sisters, these units were built at BREL, York, just a short time later between 1986 and 1987 but arrived as three-car units. Fitted with the same engines producing a top speed of 75 mph (121 kph), the seventeen units in service with First Great Western were previously operated by Wessex Trains prior to that franchise being amalgamated with FGW. The units are formed of DMSL+DMS+DM.

A fleet reshuffle in December 2006 saw eight of the units transferred to Arriva Trains Wales; FGW received an equivalent number of Class 158 DMUs as replacements. In May 2007 FGW received five Class 150/2 units under the requirements of the Remedial Plan Notice enabling the company to operate three-car Class 158 DMUs on the Portsmouth–Cardiff route. An additional five units were hired from Arriva Trains Wales in March 2010 but all had been returned by November of that year. As with their related Class 150 cousins cascaded from London Midland, they ran for a while in the green Centro/Central Trains livery; an unusual sight on Plymouth–Penzance services.

Class 153 Diesel Railcar

This class resulted from the conversion two-car Class 155 Super Sprinter DMUs (originally built between 1986 and 1988 by Leyland Bus, Workington). They were rebuilt as single-car Class 153 railcars by Hunslet-Barclay, Kilmarnock in 1991/92. Like many

Seen inside the old Reading DMU depot on 25 January 2012 is Class 150/0 unit No. 150001. Looking very smart in its fresh FGW paintwork, the unit is doing its best to cause confusion with a route blind showing Birmingham New Street via Kidderminster. The author remembers working this unit on that very route in his days as a conductor guard at Birmingham New Street. (*Courtesy of First Great Western Photo Archive*)

One of FGW's Class 150/1 DMU's No. 150128 is seen traversing the Dawlish sea wall on 20 March 2013 while forming a Plymouth–Exeter St David's service. (*Courtesy of First Great Western Photo Archive*)

Class 153 No. 153318 (at the far end of the train) having arrived at Cardiff Central with the 11:26 service from Taunton on 20 August 2012. It is being coupled to one of its Class 150/2 cousins No. 150247. (*Alun J. Caddy*)

single-car railcars they have been affectionately nicknamed 'bubble cars' by rail staff. They are classified as DMSL and intended for use on branch line work. Even so they are sometimes used to strengthen other services and during stock shortages have worked on the main line as far west as Penzance. The trains are fitted with one Cummins NT855R5 engine providing 285 hp (213 kW), giving a maximum speed of 75 mph (121 kph).

Class 158 Express Sprinter Diesel Multiple Units

The Class 158 was a completely new design of DMU and was so successful that many of them are still giving sterling service on many parts of today's UK rail network.

The Class 158/0 series of unit appeared as two-car or three-car stock, built for British Rail at BREL, Derby, between 1989 and 1992. They were intended for use on long-distance mainline local work. They were fitted with one Cummins NT855R power unit producing 350 hp (260 kW) per vehicle, giving a maximum speed of 90 mph (145 kph). Their formations were two-car DMSL(A)+DMCL and three-car DMSL(A)+MS+DMCL.

BREL, Derby, also built a variation of the class, the Class 158/9, in 1991. These two-car units were fitted with the same Cummins power units as their Class 158/0 cousins and also had a maximum speed of 90 mph (260 kW). They operated in a formation of

Class 153 Railcar No. 153318 rests between turns at Bristol Temple Meads on 7 March 2012. These units were created from modified Class 155 DMUs which were divided into two and additional cabs fitted. The new cabs were smaller than the pre-existing cab at the other end of the unit making them a little claustrophobic for some well-built drivers. (*Alun J. Caddy*)

Class 153/3 railcar No. 153370 stands at the buffers in Penzance station. Coupled to a two-car Class 150 unit it will form a service to Plymouth. All vehicles carry the 'local lines' livery of FGW. The rock in front of the train carries a welcome to visitors in both English and Cornish. (*John Balmforth*)

On 4 November 2010 Class 158/9 DMU No. 158958 is seen making the scheduled station stop at Bath while forming a Cardiff Central–Portsmouth Harbour FGW service. (*Alun J. Caddy*)

FGW Class 158/7 DMU No. 158798 is seen awaiting its next turn of duty at Cardiff Central station on 20 August 2012. (*Alun J. Caddy*)

DMSL(A)+DMSL(B). Wessex Trains had several in service and the merging into the First Great Western franchise saw transfers to the new franchise as follows:

> Class 158/0 two-car units—two units
> Class 158/0 three-car units—one units
> Class 158/9 two-car units—twelve units.

In 2008, as part of the Remedial Notice Plan, the transfer of five Class 150/2 two-car units from Arriva Trains Wales allowed FGW to create some hybrid sets by adding a single-car from the additional units to its existing Class 158/9 units, thus creating ten extra three-car trains, which considerably strengthened the Cardiff–Portsmouth, Great Malvern–Brighton, and Great Malvern–Weymouth services. Following the later transfer of Class 150/1 DMUs from London Midland and London Overground, FGW converted the remaining Class 158/0 units into three-car trains.

Class 165/1 Networker turbo units

Built as both two-car and three-car units at BREL/ABB, York, between 1992 and 1993, and introduced by British Rail for use on its Network Southeast routes, the units were fitted with one Perkins 2006 TWH power unit per vehicle. This provided three-car units with 1,050 hp (783 kW) and two-car units with 700 hp (522 kW), with a maximum speed of 75 mph (121 kph) for both types. Their formations were two-car DMCL+DMS with sixteen first class and 170 standard class seats, and three-car DMCL+ MS+DMS with sixteen first class and 270 standard class seats.

These units (numbered 165101–165117) were previously in service with Thames Trains and were absorbed into the First Great Western franchise via First Great Western Link, following boundary changes to the FGW franchise. There are sixteen of the class three-car version in service with First Great Western (165115 was scrapped after its involvement in the accident at Ladbroke Grove), and twenty in the two-car variant, all leased from Angel Trains.

Class 166 Networker Express turbo units

Like their cousins in the Class 165/1 Network Turbo Class, these three-car units were built by BREL/ABB, York, between 1992 and 1993. Introduced for use on the longer distance London Paddington–Oxford and Newbury routes, these units are all leased from Angel Trains and replaced locomotive-hauled services. They run in a formation of DMCL(A)+MS+DMCL(B).

The units are fitted with one Perkins 2006 TWH per vehicle providing 1,050 hp (783 kW) and maximum speed of 90 mph (145 kph) per train. Inherited with the absorption of the Thames Trains franchise, the units all received the First Great Western 'dynamic lines' livery in 2007 and provide thirty-two first class and 243 standard class seats.

FGW Class 165/1 Networker Turbo unit No. 165134 is seen arriving at Reading on 10 November 2011 when forming an empty stock working from the depot ready to go forward with a service to Oxford. (*John Balmforth*)

Networker Express Turbo Unit No. 166217 is greeted by passengers awaiting its arrival at Reading on 10 November 2011. The unit, wearing First Great Western 'local lines' livery, will go forward as a stopping service to London Paddington. (*John Balmforth*)

Class 175/1 Coradia 1000 Diesel Multiple Units

Built at Alstom, Birmingham, between 1999 and 2001, these new trains were among the first to be built following privatisation. FirstGroup leased them from Angel Trains for use on both its Great Western and North Western franchise services, appearing on the former wearing the FirstGroup 'Barbie' livery but later were transferred to Arriva Trains Wales. Designed for use on longer distance services, they appeared in three-car formations of DMSL(A)+MSL+DMSL(B), providing 186 standard class seats.

They are fitted with one Cummins N14 of 450 hp (335kW) per vehicle, giving a maximum speed of 100 mph (161 kph).

Class 175 Coradia unit No. 175115 emerges from Gaer tunnel, Newport, on a Bank Holiday Monday in 2005 forming the 15:30 FGW service from Cardiff Central. (*Brian Morrison*)

Class 180 Adelante five-car Diesel Multiple Units

Owned by Angel Trains the 125 mph (201kph) Class 180 Adelante trains are effectively high-speed five-car diesel multiple units used on all First Great Western main line high-speed services, but not normally west of Plymouth and Cardiff. Built between 2000 and 2002 at Alstom's Washwood Heath plant in Birmingham, they are powered by one Cummins QSK19 engine per car, giving a total of 3,750 hp (2,800 kW) per train. All have end

Scharfenberg couplings, housed behind a hinged front panel allowing units to be coupled in multiples. If a unit has to be coupled to a locomotive, a special coupler and air pipes are required. The trains operate in a formation of DMSL(A)+MFL+MSL+MSLRB+DMSL(B).

They provide forty-two first class and 226 standard class seats. Originally First Great Western had leased fourteen of the class, but with the TOC preferring to use its Class 43 HST units for long-distance work, the trains were returned to their owner, Angel Trains, from December 2007, and were ultimately transferred to other operators. However, in 2012 five of the trains were returned to First Great Western service for use on the Cotswold line, thus allowing the Class 165 and 166 units to be transferred to reinforce the Thames Valley services.

Sources: Rail Guide 2010 Colin J. Marsden (Ian Allan); Rail Guide 2013 Colin J. Marsden (Ian Allan); http://en.wikipedia.org/wiki/First_Great_Western; First Great Western.

DMU upgrades

Both the Thames Trains and West of England fleets have undergone thorough refurbishment since their transfer to First Great Western; the Thames Trains fleet received improved lighting, carpets, toilets, and revised seating layout. The programme for the West of England fleet focused on both the Portsmouth–Cardiff and West Country services, costing £11 million. The refurbishment included reupholstered seating, new lighting, new floor coverings, CCTV in the passenger saloons, and improved toilet facilities. At the same time, both fleets were repainted into the First Great Western livery, with some of the West of England units featuring artwork depicting various places of local interest.

In addition to the Thames Trains and Westfleet upgrades, the company's fleets of Class 150, Class 153, and 158 DMUs also received refurbishment. The Class 158 units underwent upgrade work at Wabtec, Doncaster, and were fitted with an additional carriage, thus converting them to three-cars, providing extra capacity. The Class 153 railcars underwent refurbishment, again by Wabtec, but this time at Eastleigh, near Southampton. The remainder of the fleet went to Pullman Rail's facility at Cardiff Canton for their refurbishment.

Future of the current fleet

It is unlikely that there will be any new trains before the present franchise ends but there is a Section 54 protection for the Class 180 Adelante units and therefore they will continue to appear until at least 2016. Leases for the remaining rolling stock currently in use will have expired by then and will require negotiation with the various owners concerning usage requirements after the new electric Super Express trains become available in 2017.

FGW Class 185 Adelante No. 185109 is seen at Great Malvern station on 29 July 2006. Led by vehicle No. 509089, of DMSL(A) type, it had been forming a London Paddington–Hereford service which on this day had terminated early at Great Malvern. (*Nigel Cripps*)

A Cardiff Central–London Paddington HST passes Undy on 28 May 2005 with Class 43 power car 43025 'Exeter' leading and No. 43130 on the rear. (*Brian Morrison*)

6

Traction Rolling Stock
Maintenance Depots

Back in the 1960s, if a young train spotter's dream was to gain access to locomotive sheds, he did so either by sneaking in unobserved or perhaps with the help of a friendly member of staff. Today that dream is virtually impossible thanks to stringent Health & Safety laws—understandable, as depots can be dangerous places for those without proper training. One thing that hasn't changed since the days of British Rail, however, is the need for top class maintenance depots to keep the railways running.

The First Great Western HST fleet forms the basis of the company's long-distance services, and at around thirty years of age it had become increasingly unreliable, requiring specialist engineering staff and depots to keep the trains running. Therefore, it's worth taking a look inside a T&RSMD.

Laira, Plymouth T&RSMD (LA)

Laira is one of the busiest of the First Great Western depots and is located a few miles to the east of Plymouth station. Its triangular shape is bounded on one side by the main A374 and the estuary of the River Plym, on another by the West of England Main Line and residential housing, while on the third side it adjoins the grounds of a college and hospital. Its origins go right back to early steam days and it was home to steam engines until March 1962, when diesel traction replaced steam. Substantial expansion took place in 1981 when a new shed, some 750 metres (2,450 feet) long, was built to accommodate the high-speed trains which would operate on the West of England Main Line. A surprising find within its boundary is a wild life reserve; this sanctuary is well preserved by First Great Western.

Colin Page, depot manager at Laira, explained that First Great Western undertakes all of its own maintenance plus some minor work for other train operating companies and has depots at the locations shown below. The depot codes and classifications are shown in brackets:
Exeter (EX)—DMUD
Laira, Plymouth (LA)—T&RSMD
Landore, Swansea (LE)—T&RSMD

Long Rock, Penzance (PZ)—T&RSMD
Old Oak Common, London (OO)—HSTMD
Oxford Carriage Sidings (OX)—CSD
Reading (RG)—DMUD
St Phillip's Marsh, Bristol (PM)—T&RSMD

When conducting research for this book I was fortunate to be granted an in-depth interview with Colin Page, who also gave me an escorted tour of the facility, so let's enjoy a visit to Laira to gain an understanding of what goes on behind its doors.

The maintenance facility at Laira is considered by First Great Western to be mainly an HST traction maintenance depot although it does provide basic overnight servicing for some other train operators, primarily through a contract with Bombardier to service around five of CrossCountry's Voyager units, and also a small number of units from First Great Western's own Westfleet, which are normally based at Bristol and Exeter. Laira does not perform the smaller 'A' examinations on the Voyager fleet. Their defects are instead classified and prioritised for the fleet owner and user. For these vehicles Laira is classed as a Notation Depot rather than full TMD, but it does have some riding inspectors that float with their experience called upon when required. During the night, two conferences take place with Bombardier to discuss any rising issues. In the daytime, only HST stock will normally be glimpsed through the windows of passing service trains at Laira, although trains which may have failed during the day sometimes find their way to the depot because of the need to keep the railway running. Laira is equipped to carry out traction and carriage examinations as follows:

- S, A & B exams—these are overnight servicing. They are classed as Level 3 examinations. Level 3 servicing is not restricted to Laira but is also carried out at other First Great Western depots.
- C & D exams—Level 4 examinations.
- E, F & G exams—these are Level 5 examinations on HST power cars, but also Levels C4 & C6 on HST trailer cars.

Whilst the various exams might well make up a large portion of the work, a lot more goes on too. This can include:

- Accident damage repairs.
- Cleaning of trains both inside and out (the depot has its own carriage wash).
- Cleaning waste from the toilet discharges; this becomes a mashed pulp clinging to the underside of the train and is not the most pleasant of jobs.
- Complete replacement of HST cabs.
- Fitting special coupling bars which enable failed HSTs to be rescued by the Thunderbird (Class 57/6) locomotives.
- Giving attention to trains that have failed in service between examinations and which have to be attended to in order to keep the services running.
- Repair and maintenance of air conditioning systems and buffet car equipment.

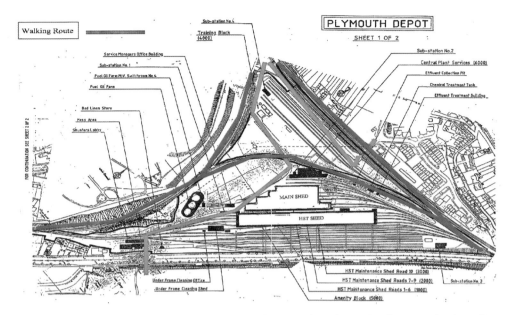

Map of the T&RSMD facility at Plymouth, Laira. The green line shows the designated safe walking routes around the depot. Interestingly, in the centre of the picture within a small triangle bounded by the red and green lines is a nature reserve. The Great Western Main Line is shown at the bottom. (*Courtesy First Great Western, Laira T&RSMD*)

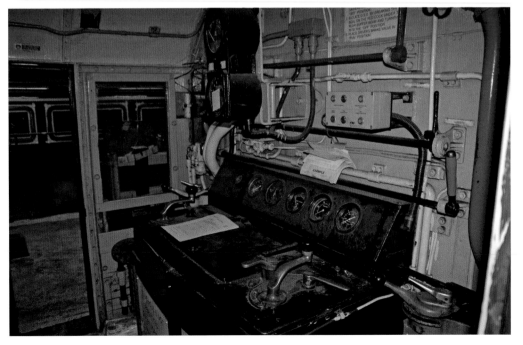

Driver's cab controls of Class 08 No. 08645 seen undergoing some remedial work at Laira T&RSMD on 24 April 2013. (*John Balmforth*)

A view not normally available to the public is the interior workings of a Class 43 power car cab. In this instance one is undergoing repair work at Laira T&RSMD. (*John Balmforth*)

A Swansea–London Paddington HST service passes Slough at speed on 25 August 2004, led by Class 43 power car No. 43122. (*Brian Morrison*)

Recently out-shopped FGW Class 43 power car No. 43004 looks very smart as it awaits its next duty at Plymouth on 21 November 2013. (*Courtesy of First Great Western Photo Archive*)

The 16:45 London Paddington–Swansea HST powers through Maes Glas, near Newport, on 28 May 2005. (*Brian Morrison*)

HST power car No. 43035 is seen plugged into the electricity supply at Laira T&RSMD , which will keep up its base air supply requirements without the need to keep its engine running. (*John Balmforth*)

The list is by no means exhaustive and is not exclusive to First Great Western since all TOCs have similar facilities available.

The depot is allocated fifty-three sets of trailer cars (427 vehicles), of which forty-nine sets are required in traffic every day—in itself no mean achievement especially since the only exceptions are Christmas Day and Boxing Day when no services operate. The depot becomes a hive of activity every night. The larger examinations at Levels 4, 5, C4 & C6 require longer stand down time and this is carefully planned. First Great Western also has 119 HST power cars shared between Laira, Old Oak Common, and Landore depots; numbers 43002–43040 are allocated to Laira. To complete such a high volume of work, Laira requires high staffing levels and, at the time of writing, has 265 people on its payroll. The depot has two HST sheds; one team works in one shed and another team in the other, but at times staff do cross and work in the other shed. Staffing grades include:

- Grade 1—Carriage cleaners
- Grade 2—Assistants
- Grade 3—Multi-skilled technicians
- Grade 4—Team Leaders
- Management grades

Colin Page explained that he considers every single one of his staff just as important as the others because without all of them working together the depot simply couldn't function. As he told me, passengers often take for granted the efforts involved in making a train run; though they will gladly complain about the standards of the train itself, for example its punctuality and cleanliness:

> It's amazing how much the importance of a dirty train is on a late running service because by being late, it gives people time to talk about it. Image is so important and our cleaning department has as much emphasis placed upon it as any other. We are clear in our minds that the cleaning department is the key to our presentation.... We are just as clear on our safety record.

There are daily team briefings, where the groups will talk about what they are going to be doing during the shift and also about any issues that may have arisen the previous day, such as service status. On top of this, managers will hold a safety and business brief once a month. The production manager will brief the shop floor staff in his domain. Cleaners have a separate presentation. Team managers have 'bolt on rules' and also hold a monthly safety and business briefing with, for instance, a cleaning department or shunting crew; all staff are included. These meetings include a local briefing which allows time to discuss whatever issues there may be. There is a Safety Committee where staff have representation from their trade union representatives. The depot manager always sits in on these, as do various safety champions. Page said, 'we have focus groups where we can try to resolve specific issues. Recently we had one concerning the safe movement of bogies.' He recognised the best way of resolving such an issue was for him to sit down with the staff who move the bogies around the depot and discuss it, which allows the company to determine exactly what the problem is and come up with a solution; the staff involved are often the best people to ask. He continued:

> It's not just a case of chucking money at it because it's often a case of having a common objective. When you have a common weight going into the pot it is easier to decide best practice. In addition to the movement of bogies on one road there is an issue with diesel fumes.

The depot conducts fume surveys but the best way of reducing fumes can just be a matter of educating people to see the need to cut down the running of engines. Again the best people to ask are the staff whose processes require an engine to be running, usually to keep up the trains air supply. There was a simple answer which was to plug the train into an electrical supply so that the air supply could be maintained without running the engines. When work is completed, instead of having to run engines for twenty to thirty minutes to get air pressure up, the base level is already there.

This shows how important it is for depot management to listen to what staff tells them, and Page feels that if they don't listen there is a risk staff will stop putting ideas forward. Equally he points out that it's important that staff understand the reason why certain things are done. Understanding this, in his opinion, leads to a high level

One of the new PIN controlled stores/tools cabinets at Laira depot is pictured on 24 April 2013. (*John Balmforth*)

An HST Mk3 First Class carriage is seen undergoing maintenance checks inside FGW's Laira T&RSMD on 24 April 2013. (*John Balmforth*)

of morale. The depot boss also feels that it is vital to get the necessary tooling sorted to enable staff to carry out their work to the high standard required. A start has been made with the introduction of tool vendors; they work on a computerised system and staff have been issued with a PIN in order to access the cabinets. They simply punch in their PIN and out comes the tool, and they return it in the same way.

> It's still not completely right yet but at least when you have tool vendors it gives traceability of certain tools, especially with IMG measuring equipment, though I accept that it is not necessarily all the equipment needed.

At the time of writing a new working group has been set up to see what is needed in the vendors:

> About 50 per cent of what's in there is for traceability purposes but is unsure if the other 50 per cent is right.
>
> I've told the staff 'You tell me what it is that frustrates you when you can't find it. What is it that puts you on the back foot at the start of your shift and thus behind for the rest of the day?' There are times when staff will say 'We want' and I have to say 'I'm sorry but we can't'. It's all about value for money and efficiency. We don't always agree but it's constructive in the sense that if it's something they don't like I can say, 'Look, people, this is the reason why.'

Turnover of staff at Laira is very low. This is a heavy engineering base and for a long time the railway had to compete with the Ministry of Defence for the workforce. Colin Page is a former MoD man himself who came out of the dockyard after serving ten years on nuclear submarines.

> I just decided I'd had enough of working with stuff that glowed in the dark. The depot staff numbers here have gone up whilst those at the MoD have gone down substantially which of course results in a high number of applicants whenever a post does become available at Laira. Vacancies are few and far between because staff simply do not want to leave resulting in a very low turnover. When I left the nuclear submarine industry I had to learn the systems specific to trains but the basic principles of engineering stand fast across both industries. Our staff understand that and it is a key to our success

Page feels that staff training could be improved; currently new employees spend their first day at the depot, and from the second day undergo a week-long corporate induction training course away from Laira, where they will learn about conflict management and the company itself. All work carried out by Laira's multi skilled technicians is safety critical, so on return to Laira they have two weeks' technical training which provides the basic minimum technical competency level, allowing them to sign off some safety-critical work such as basic exams.

Trainees then move onto their own departmental training where the rosters have built in training days supplemented by 'buddy' training. Here they are taken out onto

Class 08 No. 08410 is seen in charge of shunting manoeuvres inside Laira T&RSMD as a number of Mk3 HST carriages undergo maintenance. Note the fume extraction funnels somewhat reminiscent of steam days. (*John Balmforth*)

HST power car No. 43004 *First for the Future* photographed at London Paddington on franchise launch day 3 April 2006, in the new 'dynamic lines' vinyls. (*Brian Morrison*)

the shop floor and assessed on their competencies in different subjects with training built around that. Page feels that the technical training could be better and it is being reviewed with a lot of information gained from the twelve-monthly feedback that's done. A start has been made with the employment of two additional technical trainers and a third to handle things like the pressure washer and fork lift truck usage. Since some Westfleet work is carried out the Westfleet trainer often visits on Laira staff training days to talk about the Westfleet side. Shift teams consist of eleven members; Page says:

> We don't want eleven people in a classroom listening to one person talking about one subject because invariably if a trainee's interest is say electrical work he will pay attention but if it's not he will be constantly looking at his watch thinking about the next coffee break. We found that by ensuring no training group has more than four people we can ensure that people within the classroom are receiving training relevant to them. It's all about giving training days credibility.

With the exception of the week of corporate induction training given at the commencement of employment, all training is done at Laira's on-site training school, and the training is on-going. When a trainee asked Page when his training would be complete, he replied:

> It will never be complete because we are forever moving things along. We have a core of 70 per cent training completion but then there is the other 30 per cent where people specialise in subjects and that goes on and on. It's all about getting core principles into place and then building on that to add the specialist knowledge.

7

Named Trains Run by First Great Western*

It was traditional for British Rail, and subsequently some of the privatised train operators, to name particular services, and the tradition has been continued by First Great Western for its principal routes. In all, First Great Western still operates eighteen named trains. Those listed as follows operate Monday to Friday although some also run on Saturdays or during the summer only—timings shown were correct as of September 2013.

The Armada
(05:53 Plymouth–London Paddington)
(19:03 London Paddington–Plymouth)
The Armada is named after the Spanish fleet that sailed against England in 1588. Under the command of Lord Howard of Effingham, with Sir Francis Drake as his vice-admiral, a fleet of fifty-five warships set out from Plymouth to engage the Armada off the Eddystone Rocks.

The Atlantic Coast Express
Operates summer only.
(09:06 London Paddington–Newquay)
(15:00 Newquay–London Paddington)
The Atlantic Coast Express was first introduced by the Southern Railway in 1926, running from London Waterloo to several resorts in Devon and Cornwall. The service now operates between London Paddington and the Atlantic Coast resort of Newquay.

The Bristolian
(06:48 Weston-super-Mare–London Paddington)
(18:00 London Paddington–Bristol Temple Meads)
The Bristolian was inaugurated in 1935 by the Great Western Railway as an express service between London Paddington and Bristol Temple Meads. The name has been in use ever since.

* *Source: First Great Western.*

The Capitals United
(05:58 Swansea–London Paddington)
(16:45 London Paddington–Swansea)
The Capitals United operates between London Paddington, Cardiff Central, and Swansea. The name was originally used between 1956 and 1963 by British Railways and has been reintroduced by First Great Western to highlight the continuing importance of the rail link between the capitals of England and Wales.

The Cathedrals Express
(06:42 Hereford–London Paddington)
(18:22 London Paddington–Hereford)
The Cathedrals Express is named after the three cathedral cities on the route between London and Hereford—Oxford cathedral (established 1542), Worcester cathedral (established 743), and Hereford cathedral (established 676). The FGW train should not be confused with some privately operated steam-hauled charters that use the same title.

The Cheltenham Spa Express
(11:48 London Paddington–Cheltenham Spa)
(14:31 Cheltenham Spa–London Paddington)
The Cheltenham Spa Express runs between London Paddington and Cheltenham Spa and was named in 1923 by the Great Western Railway. It was the first train in the world to be scheduled to run at over 70 mph when, in September 1932, it covered the 77.25 miles between London and Swindon in just sixty-five minutes.

The Cornish Riviera
(10:06 London Paddington–Penzance)
(08:44 Penzance–London Paddington)
The Cornish Riviera was named after a public competition announced in the August 1904 edition of the *Railway Magazine*, the prize being three guineas (£3.15 in today's money). The name which was originally *The Cornish Riviera Limited* and referred to simply as *The Limited* by railway men and women. It has been in use since 1904, ceasing only during the two world wars. It is the oldest surviving named train in the UK.

The Cornishman
(10:00 Penzance–London Paddington)
(15:06 London Paddington–Penzance)
The Cornishman first ran in 1890 between London and Penzance and was then the fastest train in timetable to the West of England. On 20 May 1892 the train was the last broad-gauge express to depart London Paddington for Cornwall.

The Devon Express
(07:06 London Paddington–Paignton)
This service was named in 2010 to mark the launch of the new early morning service from London Paddington to the West Country. The name was chosen by children of All

Saints School, Babbacombe, Torquay, who came first in a competition held in several schools across Devon.

The Golden Hind
(05:05 Penzance–London Paddington)
(18:03 London Paddington–Penzance)
The Golden Hind operates between London Paddington and Penzance and was first introduced in the summer of 1964. The launch broke the then record for a Plymouth to London journey. The train encouraged one commuter to buy the first ever first class annual season ticket from Taunton to London Paddington.

The Mayflower
(11:06 London Paddington–Plymouth)
(15:00 Plymouth–London Paddington)
The Mayflower runs between London Paddington and Plymouth and is named after the famous ship that transported 102 pilgrims and crew from Plymouth on a sixty-six-day voyage to the new world of America in 1620.

The Merchant Venturer
(07:30 London Paddington–Penzance)
(16:00 Bristol Temple Meads–London Paddington)
The Merchant Venturer runs between London Paddington, Bristol Temple Meads, and Penzance. It is named after the Society of Merchant Venturers, a private and charitable entrepreneurial organisation that was formed in thirteenth century Bristol. In the nineteenth century the society helped to fund the building of Brunel's Clifton Suspension Bridge, and members also helped to establish the Great Western Railway.

The Night Riviera
(23:45 London Paddington–Penzance)
(21:45 Penzance–London Paddington)
The Night Riviera was named in the 1980s to compliment the Cornish Riviera day service between London Paddington and Penzance and coincided with the introduction of new air-conditioned sleeping cars.

The Pembroke Coast Express
(08:45 London Paddington–Pembroke Dock)
(10:00 Pembroke Dock–London Paddington)
The Pembroke Coast Express runs between London Paddington, Swansea, and West Wales, serving towns on and around the Pembrokeshire Coast National Park. Established in 1952, it is the only park in the UK so designated because of its spectacular coastline of rugged cliffs and sandy beaches. It covers a total area of 629 square km (240 square miles).

The Red Dragon
(07:30 Carmarthen–London Paddington)
(17:15 London Paddington–Carmarthen)
The Red Dragon runs between London Paddington and Carmarthen and is named after the mythical Red Dragon (known in Welsh as *Y Ddraig Goch*) that appears on the Welsh national flag. Although the flag was only granted official status in 1959, it is claimed to be the oldest national flag still in use, although its origins now seem to be lost in history and myth.

The Royal Duchy
(12:06 London Paddington–Penzance)
(14:00 Penzance–London Paddington)
The Royal Duchy runs between London Paddington and Penzance and is named after the Duchy of Cornwall, one of only two duchies in the UK. The eldest son of the reigning monarch inherits the title upon birth or upon his parent's accession to the throne.

The St David
(07:45 London Paddington–Swansea)
(11:28 Swansea–London Paddington)
The St David operates between Swansea and London Paddington and is named after the patron saint of Wales (in Welsh, *Dewi Sant*). St David was born sometime between 462 and 512 and was officially recognised as the patron saint of Wales in 1120.

The Torbay Express
(10:00 London Paddington–Paignton)
(14:15 Paignton–London Paddington)
The Torbay Express runs between London Paddington, Torquay, and Paignton, and was introduced by the Great Western Railway as one of its premier holiday trains to the popular resorts of Torbay.

Having just arrived at Reading with a Penzance–London Paddington service on 5 September 2011, this HST set awaits right time departure. It has already been signalled to the Main Line and will shortly follow a sister HST which has previously departed south along the slow lines. (*John Balmforth*)

A very busy scene at Reading station on 10 November 2011. The HST on the left has the route signalled to the Main Line for its journey to London Paddington—note the illuminated route indicator, sometimes wrongly called 'feathers'. Ahead another HST *en route* to Swansea is approaching as is a turbo unit which is forming a local service. Disappearing down the slope is a South West Trains Class 458 electric unit forming a service from Reading to Waterloo. (*John Balmforth*)

A First Great Western HST set headed by power car No. 43033 *Driver Brian Cooper 15 June 1947–5 October 1989* stands at the end of the line in Platform 2 at Penzance station being readied for a service back to London Paddington. The white ship in the background is the *Scillonian* waiting to ferry passengers to the Scilly Isles. (*John Balmforth*)

Trains can go no further south-west than the buffer stops under the train shed at Penzance station. Pictured here on 30 May 2012, the only means of onward travel are by air, road, or sea. (*Alun J. Caddy*)

Appendix A
Great/Greater Western Timeline and Managing Directors

1994	In BR ownership Brian Scott, Director Shadow Train Unit
1996	First Franchise 1996-2006 Franchise won by Great Western Holdings Brian Scott, Managing Director
1999	Dr Mike Mitchell, Managing Director
2000	Andy Cooper, Managing Director
2002	Mike Carroll, Managing Director Chris Kinchen-Smith, Managing Director
2004	First Great Western acquires Thames Trains (FGWL) Alison Forster, Managing Director
2006	Second Franchise 2006–2016 Greater Western won by FirstGroup Combines First Great Western/Great Western Link, Wessex Trains Alison Forster, Managing Director
2007	Andrew Haines, Managing Director
2009	Mark Hopwood, Managing Director
2013	Third Franchise to 2016

Appendix B
Main Line Routes Served by First Great Western

London Paddington	London Paddington	London Paddington	London Paddington	London Paddington
Slough	Reading	Reading	Reading	Reading
Reading	Didcot Parkway	Didcot Parkway	Didcot Parkway	Didcot Parkway
Newbury	Swindon	Swindon	Oxford	Swindon
Hungerford	Chippenham	Bristol Parkway	Hanborough	Kemble
Bedwyn	Bath Spa	Newport	Combe	Stroud
Pewsey	Bristol Temple Meads	Cardiff Central	Finstock	Stonehouse
Westbury	Weston Super Mare	Bridgend	Charlbury	Gloucester
Frome	Taunton	Swansea	Ascott-under-Wychwood	Cheltenham Spa
Bruton	Tiverton Parkway	Carmarthen	Shipton	
Castle Cary	Exeter St Davids	Fishguard Harbour	Kingham	
Taunton	Newton Abbot		Moreton-in-Marsh	
Tiverton Parkway	Totnes		Honeybourne	
Exeter St Davids	Plymouth		Evesham	
Dawlish	Liskeard		Pershore	
Teignmouth	Bodmin Parkway		Worcester Shrub Hill	
Newton Abbot	Lostwithiel		Great Malvern	
Torquay	Par		Ledbury	

Paignton	St Austell		Hereford	
	Truro			
	Redruth			
	Camborne			
	St Erth			
	Penzance			

First Great Western also operate a limited number of charter trains and in 2012 ran two to York with one of the trailer cars painted in the original InterCity livery.

Bibliography

Books

Atkins, 'Great Western Main Line Electrification', Environmental Impact Assessment, Environmental Scoping Report, (Network Rail, London, 2013)

Balmforth, John, South West Trains (Ian Allan Publishing Ltd, Hersham, Surrey, 2012)

Balmforth, John, Virgin Trains: A Decade of Progress (Ian Allan Publishing Ltd, Hersham, Surrey, 2007)

Green, Chris & Mike Vincent, The InterCity Story 1964–2012 (Oxford Publishing Company, Hersham, Surrey, 2013)

Harris, Nigel (ed.), The Comprehensive Guide to Britain's Railways 2011 (Bauer Media, Peterborough, 2011)

Jones, Robin, Brunel's BIG Railway (Motions Media Group Ltd, Horncastle, Lincolnshire, 2013)

Marsden, Colin J., Rail Guide 2013, (Ian Allan Publishing Ltd, Hersham, Surrey, 2013)

Marsden, Colin J., Rail Guide 2010, (Ian Allan Publishing Ltd, Hersham, Surrey, 2010)

Marsden, Colin J., Traction Recognition 2007 (Ian Allan Publishing Ltd, Hersham, Surrey, 2007)

Websites

www.firstgreatwestern.co.uk/About-Us/Our-Business (accessed 28/07/2013)

www.firstgreatwestern.co.uk/Your-journey/Rail-improvements/Reading-station (accessed 28/07/2013)

www.firstgreatwestern.co.uk/About-Us/Our-business/Performance (accessed 28/07/2013) http://en.wikipedia.org/wiki/Great_Western_Trains (accessed 31/07/2013)

www.firstgroup.com/corporate/latest_news (accessed 28/07/2013)

www.walesonline.co.uk/news/business (accessed 31/07/2013)

http://en.wikipedia.org/wiki/GRT_Group (accessed 22/09/2013)

http://en.wikipedia.org/wiki/Great_Western_Trains (accessed 31/07/2013)

http://en.wikipedia.org/wiki/Wessex_Trains (accessed 31/07/2013)